REALISM IN EDUCATION

HARPER'S SERIES ON TEACHING

Under the Editorship of Ernest E. Bayles

REALISM IN EDUCATION

WM. OLIVER MARTIN
University of Rhode Island

HARPER & ROW, PUBLISHERS

New York, Evanston, and London

REALISM IN EDUCATION

Copyright © 1969 by Wm. Oliver Martin. Printed in the United States of America. All rights reserved. No part of this book may be used or reproduced in any manner whatsoever without written permission except in the case of brief quotations embodied in critical articles and reviews. For information address Harper & Row, Publishers, Incorporated, 49 East 33rd Street, New York, N.Y. 10016.

Library of Congress Catalog Card Number: 69–18490

Editor's Foreword	vii
Preface	ix
1. A Realistic and Phenomenological Analysis of the Teaching-Learning Activity	1
2. Immediate and Remote Ends in Teaching and Learning	19
3. The Material Cause: Some Moral Relations Between Teacher and Student	58
4. Knowledge as the Formal Cause in Teaching and Learning	82
5. The Curriculum and Efficient Causation	148
Index	195

Editor's Foreword

The purpose, presumably, of stocking the mind is to secure retrieval of any one of the stored items when it is wanted. And, like a well-ordered library, retrieval is readily possible only when a well-ordered and easily understood filing system is in effect. Any worker who understands the system can then, at any time, go straight to a desired item, even though its location or even its existence was previously unknown to him. Logical deduction, not memory, serves as the locational principle.

Thought patterns represent the filing systems of the mind. To be able to "follow the run" of a thought pattern is to understand it. Broad principles or generalizations—high-level abstractions—constitute thought patterns that have high retrieval value; they represent the kind of knowledge that makes transfer readily possible and enables a possessor to find it useful. The only genuinely practical subject-matter content a teacher can teach is basic, tested theory. And to think of philosophy as something other than broad, basic theory is probably to lose for philosophy any legitimate claim to a significant place in education.

Of extant philosophical systems, which furnishes the best organizational base for educational practice? This question is vital for an educational philosopher, and it seemingly should be of first importance for an educational practitioner. Chesterton, when asked whether it is important for a landlady to know a prospective tenant's philosophy of life, countered with the question, "Is anything else important?" This book is one in a series designed to furnish authentic presentations of major contemporary philosophies as they relate to, or impinge upon, educational practice. Each book takes a given philosophy and follows it into its impact or impacts upon such practice. Each author is presumed to be sympathetic to the view he presents and able to speak authoritatively for it. What each philosophy has to offer for education should therefore be discernible in the book devoted to it. Although the general editor and the publisher have not tried to tell any author how he should write his book, they are hopeful that this end will be served.

In addition, publication of the series in the form of separate paperbacks offers flexibility and economy in classroom use: An instructor is thus able thereby to select the specific views he wants studied, whether one or several, and require student purchases of those. Each book in the set is written with the expectation that the others will also be available—hence with no obligation to present any view but its own, even with the necessity perhaps, because of space limitation, to deal with that alone. We hope that the books in this series will prove highly useable and useful.

Ernest E. Bayles

PREFACE

The term "realism" is somewhat ambiguous, especially when used in reference to the philosophy of education. Does the term refer to one among many positions, the choice of which is determined by the "temperament" of the chooser? Or, does the term refer to a position which, when fully developed and understood, is the "truest," and to which other "viewpoints" are recognized as partial truths? It is my conviction that only the latter does justice to authentic realism.

From Aristotle to A. N. Whitehead, if one wishes to probe in depth into the "nature of things," in contrast to a merely "horizontal" or superficial approach—and there is no strong either-or here, for both are necessary—then one must come to grips with the traditional, and famous, four causes. This, we shall attempt to do; not adequately, of course, in the space allowed us, but in part.

Our approach to the philosophy of education will be to ask what is the nature, the structure, of the teaching-learning activity. In such a structure the four causes—material, formal, efficient, and final—will be found, not because we *posit* that they must be there, but rather because *there they are*.

Statistically speaking, most writings on education today are on a very practical level, dealing especially with the impact of contemporary technology, directly and indirectly, on formal schooling. This is both necessary and good, but it is not sufficient. Education is bound to be affected, from kindergarten through the university, by the various kinds of change now taking place. Such change may be understood, in part, by many kinds of analyses—economic, political, psychological, and sociological. But all of these analyses, by their very nature, have philosophical presuppositions which, again, by their very nature, are outside their province. And it is not always clear, when conclusions are reached, whether they are independent, as facts, of philosophical presuppositions, or that they are merely deductions from them. In the latter case, the conclusions would *appear* to be "empirical," but would really be only deductions from a philosophical position assumed, but for which no evidence is given.

It is the purpose of this study to search, if only in a limited way, for those philosophical truths in terms of which all educational means, i.e., practice, should be guided. Such truths, principles, are also those in terms of which any given "education-claims" should be judged.

It may be a welcome surprise to those educators not very familiar with the philosophy of education as a discipline to know that a great deal of very high-level work has been produced in the last twenty-five years. This is in contrast to the same number of years before World War II, when so much of what passed for the philosophy of education was more ideological than philosophical. One reason for the contrast, but only in part, has been the development of "analysis" as a method, whether linguistic or logical.

The author recognizes his debt to this and other philosophical developments, and to the many workers in the philosophy of education. Since few names are mentioned in our study, which aims to be more analytical than polemical, this needs to be emphasized.

Wm. Oliver Martin

Kingston, Rhode Island

1

A REALISTIC AND PHENOMENOLOGICAL ANALYSIS OF THE TEACHING-LEARNING ACTIVITY

If the teaching process is structured, then we can speak of an "order of teaching." The same may be said for "learning." Now the question may be asked: What pattern of order can be discovered in the teaching and learning activity that is independent of time, place, or circumstances?

Before proceeding further, this question raises others. Is there any reality to which the question can be referred? Is there some "teaching essence" that in a Platonic fashion floats around externally related to, hence untouched by, time, place, or circumstances? Probably not. But even if it were so, then have we not already assumed that which later will be said to have been discovered? The answer must be in the negative. What we assume is that which makes communication possible. All teaching, anywhere, has certain common characteristics; otherwise the term "teaching" would be so equivocal as to be meaningless.

No abstract "teaching essence" is assumed, if by that is meant that the task we have set for ourselves is merely one of elaborating on some a priori definition. This would be game playing and, from the standpoint of intelligent communication, all discussion would be limited to the matter of logical consistency, and not to that of truth.

Rather, the approach should be an experiential one. By the use of philosophical analysis and the phenomenological method, the teaching process can be described and understood. Teaching has a structure *about which* there may be theories, but the structure cannot be deduced from a theory. This quite legitimate kind of priority can be applied to other areas.

To illustrate. In an analysis of "authority," independently of all speculation, the locus of all authority lies in a person or persons, and not in any subhuman object such as, say, a book. When we speak of a book in physics as "authoritative," it is a manner of speaking. It is really the author who is the authority. Again, in understanding justice we make the distinction between *being* just and *acting* justly. One may be essentially a just person and yet at times act unjustly. On the other hand, it may be said of another that he is an unjust person by nature and habit, and yet he may at times do just acts.

In these two examples no arbitrary a priori assumptions are made. Furthermore, all theory and speculation must rest upon these distinctions which constitute "hard data." Likewise, similar distinctions constituting hard data should be discernible in an analysis of the teaching and learning process.

Now, granting all this, one might ask of what importance is the basic question or problem we have posed. The answer is, that to the degree that we know the structure of something, or the pattern of order of a process, then we know to some extent *what* it is. All determination is negation, and conversely; hence to know what teaching is, we must know what it is not, and conversely. If I know that nothing nonpersonal can be an authority, then I can avoid false loci of authority and can also better understand corruptions of it. And so, to the degree that I understand what teaching must be in order to be what it is, then I can better understand what appears to be, but is not teaching, and can also recognize kinds of corruption of it.

At the end of this chapter we shall show the power of analysis in clarifying a problem that seems to be a matter of endless debate, e.g., the question of whether one should primarily teach children or teach subject matter.

It should be noted that the question we posed, and to which we shall presently respond, does not require a discussion of the relevance of the psychological or sociological aspects in education. However, these are relevant to other questions and problems in education, for all teaching and learning take place in a social milieu.

THE TEACHING RELATION AS TRIADIC

Whatever else teaching may be, it is at least a relation. A *person*, T, teaches *something* to another *person*, S. Analogous notions of teaching, where the nonpersonal is involved, are not relevant to this educational problem, e.g., a mother cat teaching a kitten, or a person teaching a dog to do tricks. In the phenomenological description of teaching the aim is to discover "what is there." Now, what kind of a relation do we find? It is a triadic relation, having three terms—the person who teaches, the person who is taught, and what is taught, i.e., some kind of knowledge. The relation is similar to that of "giving," and dissimilar to that of, say, "pushing." Peter gives X to Paul. Essential to this relation is the giver, that which is given, and the person to whom the object is given. "Pushing" is a diadic relation, and hence one can say that "Peter pushes Paul" because only the two terms are involved. But one cannot literally say, "Peter gives Paul," for that would not be intelligible without an answer as to what is given. Even in the context of marriage, when it is said that the "father gives his daughter," the latter is *that which* is given, not the person who is the receiver.

It may be observed that, although all this is true for a triadic relation such as "giving," nevertheless "teaching" seems to be used in the same way as a relation like "pushing," which is diadic. Just as we can say that Peter pushes Paul, can't we say that Peter teaches Paul? Yes, we can, but it takes only a little more observation to understand that the similarity is only in the "manner of speaking," not in the relations themselves. In the diadic relation of "pushing," *what* is pushed is the same as the person *who* is pushed; whereas in "teaching," what is taught is not the same as the person *who* is taught.

It is the fact that what is taught is some kind of knowledge that makes the teaching relation triadic. Just as there cannot be a giver without a gift, so there can be no teacher without the possibility of some kind of knowledge, *that which* is taught.

Although all of this may be true, its significance may not be apparent. Suffice it to say at present that, so far from being a trivial matter, the understanding of teaching to be a triadic relation is necessary to the understanding of the denial of, or corruption of, teaching. Later we shall see that "indoctrination" in the "bad" sense of the term, is defined by the reduction of teaching to a diadic relation.

The teaching relation may be formalized in the following way: T (the teacher) teaches K_1 (some kind of knowledge) to S (the student).

Since there must be some end or purpose in any act of teaching, and also some means by which the teaching takes place, the teaching relation may be formalized further in this way: T teaches K_1 to S, by (means of) M, and for (the end) E.

It is to be observed that teaching does not cease to be a triadic relation merely because M and E are always presupposed. The relation of "giving" does not cease to be triadic because a gift must be given by some means, by hand or by mail. Nor does "pushing" cease to be a diadic relation because it is done by hand or with a pole, and for some purpose.

KNOWLEDGE AS WHAT IS TAUGHT

It is a person *who* is taught by another person, a teacher. *What* is taught is knowledge of some kind. The term "knowledge," from the standpoint of teaching, can be thought of as having the widest possible meaning for educational purposes. It includes the theoretical and the practical kinds of knowledge, the know-how, the know-what, and the know-why. One can teach another mathematics, physics, philosophy, how to paint a picture, build a bridge, play chess, fish for trout, wire a house, repair a doorbell, or lift a heavy object.

Now the question must be asked: Is that which can be taught the same as, and coextensive with, that which can be known or learned? There would seem to be at least four classes of cases in which a person can learn something without being taught by a teacher.

There is a kind of knowledge acquired by intuition or by acquaintance. A person knows what pain is by acquaintance. He either knows what pain is, or he doesn't. There is little that a teacher can do. Rather, knowledge of what is pain is something which a teacher makes use of in teaching a person something else. To have knowledge by acquaintance, a teacher is not only unnecessary, but it may well be that such knowledge cannot be taught. It should be noted that, however necessary knowledge by acquaintance is in the learning process, from the standpoint of the whole educational process it is relatively trivial. There would be a confusion of necessity with rank of value if this distinction were not admitted. In the process of living nothing is so necessary as breathing for the human being. Yet in rank of value it is the ultimate in triviality.

Second, there is the ordinary kind of knowledge that comes from direct experience and which does not require a teacher. A wife does not need a teacher to know the habits of her husband. One does not need a teacher to know that in New York City there is relatively heavy traffic. For this ordinary kind of knowledge it is conceivable that a teacher might be helpful, but in any case certainly not necessary.

Third, there is another kind of knowing and learning gained by trial and error. If this is a part of controlled experimentation, then it is a part of what presently we shall call "research." Otherwise, learning by trial and error without a teacher is simply to rediscover for oneself what is probably already known. This is learning by "doing it the hard way." For example, one might learn to bowl fairly well without a teacher. However, it is more efficient to learn through a teacher whatever is known and can be a part of a body of knowledge.

Fourth, there is another kind of learning and knowing that cannot wholly be taught by any teacher, namely, research work. A research worker who has discovered some new truth, and hence has added this to our knowledge, can say that he has learned something that could not have been taught to him. Before his research work no teacher had the new knowledge, and hence could not have taught it. To illustrate in a rather simple manner, a teacher could not have taught Einstein that $E = mc^2$, for such knowledge was not known. By his work Einstein discovered a new truth. His knowing and learning in this case was the same, and took place without the necessity of, or the possibility of, a teacher.

When it is said that a person is taught by a teacher, the teacher may or may not be immediately present. For example, learning mathematics "on one's own" is still a case of being taught by a teacher. The teacher is not immediately present in a school. Nevertheless, the teacher is the author of the book being studied by the student.

A summary statement can now be made in terms of the following propositions:

1. Knowledge by acquaintance and by intuition, and also knowledge obtained by direct experience, cannot be taught but is presupposed in the teaching of any other kind of knowledge.

2. The kind of knowledge obtained by trial and error is possible without a teacher. For such knowledge a teacher may not be necessary, but one learns more efficiently with a teacher.

3. In the case of new knowledge obtained through research work

a teacher is necessary, but not sufficient. Without having been taught, the new knowledge discovered by the research worker would not have been possible. Yet the new knowledge, precisely because it is something new, could not have been taught.

The importance of teaching is evident. Other than the primitive and ordinary experiences—which one may have before schooling, and also may have with or without schooling—whatever a person knows is the result of having been taught, directly or indirectly. It may be observed that schooling presupposes a teacher, but that the converse is not the case. A parent can teach a child some kind of knowledge. In practice, however, especially in our contemporary civilization, the relevance of the distinction is questionable. In fact the relevance of the distinction decreases in significance as a person approaches the secondary and university level of education.

It would seem, then, that on the level of higher education whatever a student is to learn and to know is that which he must be taught. The only exception would be the new knowledge discovered in research work. But even for this, knowledge already known and taught by teachers is presupposed. With respect to the new knowledge obtained through research work the university can do little other than provide the conditions for the discovery of such new knowledge, leaving it to the individual workers to make such knowledge a reality.

Common to all schooling, from the elementary through the university level, is the teaching function. Yet what distinguishes higher education, especially the university, is the fact that part of its function is to establish conditions for research work to be done in order that new knowledge may be obtained. Is, then, the research work the most important function of the university, to which the teaching function is merely an instrumental means relatively not on the same level or rank of value? This can hardly be the case when we realize that research work need not be done in a university, but can be done outside of it. An example would be the research work done by industry. Industry presupposes of necessity the teaching function of a university, even though it may itself supplement such teaching. It does not in the same way presuppose the research function of the university. Although such a research function is desirable from the standpoint of industry, it does not presuppose its necessity in the sense that it does presuppose the necessity of the university's teaching function.

In the light of this understanding it may be said that the teaching function of a university is relatively the most important, the term "important" referring in this case not so much to "rank of value," but rather to that which is necessary in contrast to that which is desirable.

THE TEACHING RELATION AS ASYMMETRICAL

If T teaches K_1 to S, then the converse would be that S learns K_1 from T. In this case the converse is different, and hence the relation is said to be asymmetrical. A relationship is symmetrical if aRb implies bRa. It would seem, then, that the teaching relation is asymmetrical, for the teacher-student relationship cannot both be and not be at one and at the same time. However, the question of symmetry in connection with the diadic relation does not quite do justice to a triadic relation, and hence we shall see that a few qualifications are necessary.

1. A question may be raised about the relationship of teaching to learning. Can a teacher teach a certain kind of knowledge and the student not learn anything of that knowledge? It would seem that a negative answer must be given. For teaching to occur, the kind of knowledge taught must be in some sense the same as the kind of knowledge learned.[1] Of course, what is actually learned

[1] In an excellent essay ("Two Senses of 'Learn,'" *Oregon Higher Education*, June, 1963) Dr. Alburey Castell distinguishes between two senses of the word "learn." He says: "In one sense, we use the word 'learn' to refer to what happens when a person acquires, retains, and is about to reproduce or repeat. In *this* sense you can learn that $2 + 2 = 5$, or that the earth is shaped like a cube." (p. 1) "But there is another sense, namely 'getting to know' or 'liquidating ignorance.' These two senses are not the same, and I see no advantage in glossing over the difference." (p. 1)

Needless to say, when we speak of learning, we are referring to it in the latter sense, although in practice undoubtedly it is always a little mixed with learning, sense I. One only approaches learning, sense I, in its purity when, as we shall see later, the teaching relation is reduced from a triadic to a diadic relation.

may be only a small part of what the teacher attempted to teach. For teaching to exist actually, and not merely potentially, the student must learn something of the kind of knowledge that is being taught. Degrees of perfection in teaching must be admitted. However, if the student learns nothing of the kind of knowledge being taught, then the substance of teaching does not exist, only the appearances and the empty forms. If a student in chemistry literally never learns anything from his immediate teacher present in person, nor from his remote teacher, the author of the textbook, then it seems reasonable to say, whatever else they may have been doing, that neither teacher taught him chemistry. Can a woodchopper work at being a woodchopper and at the same time there be no cuts on the tree? In the case of a triadic relation such as "giving," if B never received X from A, then it surely can be said that, whatever his intentions and acts, A did not give X to B.

2. Let us suppose that teaching as an asymmetrical relation is denied and the relation is called symmetrical. In this case T teaches K_1 to S implies that S teaches K_1 to T, and hence that, presumably, T learns K_1 from S. The existential contradiction is apparent, for it is impossible to teach K_1 to S unless T already knows it; and if so, then he could not have learned it from S.

The understanding of the teaching relation as asymmetrical is not at all changed by the fact that, if the temporal process is considered, then in the order of being the teacher-student relationship may be reversed. Peter, a ninth-grade teacher, may teach algebra to Paul. Paul later gets a Ph.D. degree in mathematics, becomes a professor, and finds Peter, his high school teacher, now a student. In this example, the knowledge referred to is mathematics, but it is not wholly the same knowledge in both cases. Rather it is some specific aspect of mathematics as a kind of knowledge. Peter taught algebra to Paul, and Paul later taught differential equations to Peter. But one cannot say that, if Peter teaches algebra to Paul, it follows that Paul teaches algebra to Peter. But one can say that Paul learns algebra from Peter.

It is sometimes said humorously that a teacher learns a lot from his students. Of course, properly interpreted, this is true. But it does not alter the asymmetry of the teaching relation, it really presupposes it. In teaching logic one may learn that not everyone has the same ability to think clearly—a psychological fact. But what the teacher teaches is not the same knowledge as what he (the teacher) may learn from the act of teaching. One cannot formally teach something if that which is taught is never learned. But it is possible to learn something without being formally taught.

We may note that there is a eulogistic sense in which a great contemporary teacher may, in a book, say that he has learned a great deal from his students. But in reality this charitable statement is possible only if the actual teacher-student relationship is presupposed. The reader should never be so naive as to assume that the author of the book literally meant that both he and the student were on the same level, and that each taught each other in the same sense a specific kind of knowledge.

3. Let us take the case of a teacher teaching mathematics (M) to a student doing research work for a doctorate. If, through such work, some new knowledge is discovered by the student, and hence is known and learned by the teacher, cannot it be said that in this case the teacher-student relationship becomes symmetrical? If the teacher teaches M to S, then at least in this case it seems that S teaches M to T also, which is the simple converse making the teacher relation symmetrical. But appearance is still not reality, for again the "M" is not the same in each case. The converse is different because there is a change from M_1 to M_2. The mathematics taught and the mathematics learned are not the same.

The advanced student may also be a teacher, and in a seminar the teacher may be said to learn from the advanced student. But it is still true that if Peter teaches M_1 to Paul, and Paul teaches M_2 to Peter, that the teaching relation is asymmetrical.

With all of these qualifications and distinctions we can now understand the one case in which the teaching relation can be said to appear symmetrical, namely, the case in which a kind of knowledge is referred to as a whole and in relation to another kind of knowledge, and not with respect to the whole in relation to its parts. In the process of participating in a series of high-level seminars, Peter and Paul may learn mathematics from each other, and hence each may be said to have taught the other. With respect to the parts or aspects of mathematics, the teaching relation is still asymmetrical. But if a kind of knowledge, in this case mathematics, is considered not in relation to its parts or aspects, but rather in its unity as one kind of knowledge in relation to other kinds of knowledge, then may not the teaching relation be said to be symmetrical?

If T teaches M_1 to S, one can say that S may teach M_2 to T, meaning that the person who in the one case is a student relative to the person who is teaching him, may also become a teacher of that very same person if either the kind of knowledge is different or, in the case of the same kind of knowledge, the aspect is different. However, we do not speak in the same manner when a relation is truly symmetrical. The relation "next to" is symmetrical. If A is next to B, then B *must* be, not merely *may* be, next to A. But, if Peter teaches mathematics to Paul, we cannot say that it must be the case that Paul teaches mathematics to Peter. Even the drop in modality from "must" to "may" is possible only among those who are professionals in a field of knowledge, and hence are approximately equals with respect to other people, the students in the school who are not teachers. Even when Peter and Paul may be said to learn from each other, and hence teach each other, *they are teachers not because of the relation they have to each other, but rather by virtue of the relation they have to the student body*. With reference to the possibility of teachers teaching each other, the teaching relation may be said to be nonsymmetrical.

In any case in which there is a change on the level of knowledge, M_1 to M_2, then in the order of being there is a change in who is teaching whom. Peter teaches M_1 to Paul; Paul, in his research work, discovers M_2, which Peter learns. Nevertheless, the asymmetrical relation still holds. If Peter teaches M_1 to Paul, then the converse must be that Paul learns M_1 from Peter, all of which is quite compatible with the fact that Paul teaches M_2 to Peter.

In summation, we may state the following three principles: (a) If the kind of knowledge is the same, then the relation of teacher and student can be reversed only if there is a change in the aspect of the knowledge which is referred to. This occurs essentially in research work; any other case would be accidental. (b) The teacher-student relationship can be reversed if the kind of knowledge referred to is different. (c) If both the kind of knowledge and the aspect are the same, then the teacher-student relationship must be asymmetrical.

THE TEACHING RELATION AS TRANSITIVE

We have seen that the teaching relation is triadic and asymmetrical. Is it also transitive, or intransitive? A relation is transitive if it is such that aRb and bRc implies aRc. The relation "above" is transitive, the relation "father of" is intransitive. At first sight it would seem that the teaching relation must be intransitive. If Peter teaches a certain kind of knowledge, K_1, to Paul, and Paul teaches K_1 to John, then one cannot say that therefore Peter teaches K_1 to John. Or can one? If one so argued in the case of the relation "father of," he could be accused of equivocation, or of "word play." The "grandfather" relation is not the same as the "father" relation.

Now, of course, this is true. But there are several considerations that must be taken into account.

1. The relations "above" and "father of" are diadic relations. The "teaching" relation is triadic, as we have seen. This difference may be a relevant fact when considering the question of transitivity. Of course, a question can be raised in the theory of relations as to whether it makes any sense to speak of a triadic relation as either transitive or intransitive. Perhaps there is no answer except that which is discovered through an experiential approach.

2. We have already seen that a distinction must be made between the immediate teacher who is present before the student, and the remote teacher who is not present in person but indirectly by means of a book, which may be a group of "classical writings," (e.g., Plato), or a textbook, or a record or tape recording. Another distinction relevant to transitivity is that between knowledge and the existential. With respect to the existential, i.e., Peter, Paul, and John, the teaching relation is intransitive or nontransitive depending upon whether Peter is dead or alive. If Peter is alive, then the relation is nontransitive, for Peter may or may not be the immediate teacher of John. If Peter is dead, having died before

or during the time when Paul taught John, then the relation is intransitive.

3. These very real distinctions have been made because, in a triadic, as opposed to a diadic, relation, there are two points of reference in analyzing transitivity. However, in terms of relevance, one of the points of reference, the knowledge taught is the most important in understanding the teaching process, and not the existential accident of who is alive or dead, immediate or remote. With respect to knowledge the teaching relation is transitive, without regard to whether Peter is alive, dead, or remote. This fact is all the more understandable if one looks upon teaching not as a static but as a dynamic relation, as a continual cultural process requiring, in all but primitive forms, organizational institutions.

Paul teaches John analytical geometry. Now there is a sense in which it may be said that Paul has learned M_1 (analytical geometry) from Descartes, and hence it can be said that Descartes has taught M_1 to Paul. Therefore, it may be said that, by a continuity of the cultural process—including institutions (schools), printing presses, etc.—Descartes teaches M_1 to John. If other than the present teachers are taken into account, then the teaching relation must be transitive, for were it not for the remote teachers there could be no knowledge conserved and passed on, and hence nothing for a present teacher in person to teach.

4. In a triadic relation such as teaching, what makes possible the relation of transitivity is the mediating factor, the knowledge that is transmitted. A diadic relation has no such mediating factor; and hence, in the case of (say) "father of," it would be not only word-play but also quite false to say that if A is the father of B, and B is the father of C, then A is the father of C. However, for the reasons given, the teaching relation can be said to be transitive, because the truth lies not in the "manner of speaking," but rather has its foundation in the very real cultural process in which and through which teaching takes place.

In passing, it may be noted that in the very nature of the teaching relation as transitive, which helps make possible the cultural process, there is also an existential mediating factor, namely, Paul. By using a category of the order of being, metaphysics, we may analogically think of a kind of knowledge as an "essence." If so, there is already a hint as to what can happen to the teaching relation in terms of an existentialism in which essence is denied.

It is because a kind of knowledge is the mediating factor that the teaching relation is transitive; and not conversely. This fact can be described in the following way:

1. The kind of knowledge, K_1, must be a specific kind of knowledge. (a) One cannot teach in general or teach knowledge in general. Rather one always teaches something specific. (b) Were it not the case that something specific is taught, there could be no question of evidence bearing upon the truth or falsity of propositions. For one does not gather "evidence in general."

2. The K_1 taught by Peter to, and learned by, Paul must be the same, at least in part, with the K_1 which Paul teaches to, and is learned by, John. (a) What Paul learns of K_1 may be only a part of the K_1 Peter tries to teach. It is also possible for Paul to learn something *about* K_1, and *in* K_1, which Peter did not deliberately try to teach. (b) No remote end can be a substitute for the immediate end or purpose in teaching. Otherwise the continuity in teaching is destroyed because the mediating factor, a kind of knowledge, is indirectly denied. Paul learns about wrestling from his teacher, Peter, and is hired as a coach to teach John. But Paul is more interested in "teaching" the morality of sports, and acts accordingly. In such a case John is likely to learn very little of wrestling or morality. This is not to deny that if wrestling is properly taught, some knowledge of, and perhaps practice in, character development may also be learned. However, the correct causal order must be respected. An apple tree produces blossoms because it primarily produces apples; and not conversely. If, through some biological perverseness, the tree were to invert the causal priority, then it would produce nothing at all.

SOME IMPLICATIONS OF THE DENIAL OF THE THREE CHARACTERISTICS

It would take a good-size book to deal fully with the implications that the three characteristics have for educational process, from the elementary school through the university. Of equal interest are the implications which come from the denial of teaching as a relation characterized as triadic, asymmetrical, and transitive—the latter two, of course, having been carefully defined. Some of these implications may now be briefly stated.

One way of destroying or corrupting the teaching relation would be to reduce it to a diadic relation. This occurs when the notion is upheld that one teaches primarily not subject matter but the child. An argument then ensues as to which is best, a subject matter centered or a child centered school.

We have already seen that, in a manner of speaking, we can say that a teacher teaches a student. But, if it is taken literally, then instead of T teaches K_1 to S we would have to say T "teaches" S. The quotation marks are necessary in order to distinguish word from concept. The word "teaches" now refers to a completely different concept, one such as "determines," or "manipulates." These are really diadic relations. And so is the term "brainwash."

What, then, happens to the pattern of order expressed by "T teaches K_1 to S, by (means of) M, and for (the end) E"? The whole formula collapses. The end "E" must now be interpreted in terms of social adjustment and the avoidance of maladjustment. The intellect must be reduced to "intelligence" as an instrument of adjustment. (And the "will" must be reinterpreted as a function of "interest," etc.)

What happens, then, to K_1, a kind of knowledge to be taught? It is shifted over to the means, M. A kind of knowledge can no longer mean an immaterial assimilation of a pattern of order to be found in "the nature of things." In fact, there can literally be no kinds of knowledge, for even knowledge has to be reinterpreted in social and functional terms as a means of adjustment. No longer does the order and nature of knowledge limit and help to determine pedagogical means. The converse is the case, and hence pedagogy ceases to be a means by which the student is taught a kind of knowledge; rather it becomes a means of "teaching" which now refers to a means of *manipulating* the student.

The distinction between the order of knowledge and that of the order of teaching and learning has also vanished. Categories of knowledge are gradually reduced to institutional categories. For example, philosophy as a kind of knowledge and as wisdom fades away and, in so far as the name is still retained, is to be found as one among the "humanities"—a term standing not for a kind of knowledge, but rather a term created for institutional (university) purposes. Institutional categories are necessary, but they must be founded upon, or at least be compatible with, the order of knowledge—just as the order of knowledge must have its foundation in the order of being. Otherwise, concepts, propositions, and arguments cease to have a truth-function, as instruments *by which* we know *what* things are and because of this also have a use function. Rather, the converse is the case, and ideology becomes supreme.[2]

The total corruption of teaching can be carefully defined, but in practice it would be difficult to find. In reality there are usually only asymptotic approaches, the teaching relation being reduced to a diadic relation the least in mathematic and physics, but more so in what are called the "social sciences" and the "humanities."

Finally, a few remarks about asymmetry and transitivity. Legitimate authority, which a teacher *qua* teacher should have, has its foundation in the relation of asymmetry. With respect to the kind of knowledge being taught, the teacher and the student are unequal. The relationship cannot be reversed. However, the reversal can be approached asymptotically, if, and only if, through acquisition of knowledge, and hence through *merit*, the student tends to become equal to his teacher. With respect to institutional purposes, i.e.,

---

[2] The term "ideology" has a history, of course. But we are not concerned with philology. Professor H. D. Aiken, in speaking of the 19th century as the "Age of Ideology," states quite accurately what ideology is in contrast to philosophy, i.e., metaphysics. The function of ideologies is to "enable us to organize our energies more adequately for the satisfaction of our total needs as men. Then they will be 'true' in the only sense of the term which is worth considering." (*The Age of Ideology: The 19th Century Philosophers*, Mentor, 1956, p. 270) Furthermore, whether an ideology is "cognitive" or not is unimportant, according to Professor Aiken.

If there is no order of being, then there is no order of knowledge. And if there is no order of knowledge, then there is no order of teaching and learning. And if there is no order of teaching and learning, then "teaching" becomes "determining" or "manipulating" for individual and/or social purposes. Hence, there are no principles of human thought and action, which is identical with saying, as Professor Aiken does, that such ". . . principles are rooted, in the end, only in our commitment to them . . ." (p. 274) in so far as schooling is concerned, when the student becomes so advanced, as a graduate student or as a research worker, that he approaches in knowledge the level of the teacher, then the teacher-student relationship tends to vanish. The student is pushed out of his academic nest to fly for himself. The student may now become a teacher, a colleague—but he can earn his status and right only through merit, through the mastery of some kind of knowledge.

If the denial of asymmetry implies the denial of the authority of the present, living teacher, the denial of transitivity does the same for the authority of the teachers and scholars of the past. Historicism tends to blur over the distinction between truths which are revelant to, because dependent upon, a given era, and those truths which are revelant to the same era precisely *because* they transcend it. In this case, utility tends to become a substitute for the truth relation, and usefulness is determined in terms of present and future interests. For example, under the guise of the "Democratic way of life," which in effect is an euphemism for a "doctrinal skepticism" as regards knowledge, the teacher may be reduced to a guide in looking up "resource material." Through something called "consensus theory" the teacher may be reduced to a poll taker.

It is said that we see further because we stand on the shoulders of our forefathers. This is true. The foundation of this is the transitive relation as a characteristic of teaching. Teaching takes place in, but is not bound to, the present. In contrast to "search" and "research," teaching has essentially a conservative function. All that which is now taught and learned was once new. Such knowledge is the actuality we must conserve, and which makes possible the potentially new knowledge of the future.

It will be seen that the order of teaching and learning, as thus far developed, reflect the traditional four causes. And this is as it should be if there are only the four ultimate kinds of causes. The approach, however, has been experiential rather than a priori. In the latter case, one would start with the material, efficient, formal, and final causes, and then look for their proper exemplifications in the teaching-learning activity. The danger here is that of "imposing" a metaphysical order upon a human activity without first considering and describing *what* it is. In the case we have taken, what the teaching-learning structure is, is first discovered and described; and then it is *discovered* that the structure can be correlated with, and understood in terms of, the four causes. This will be the task of the following chapters, and it is hoped that what has not been said will not radically change what has been said.

The most realistic approach is phenomenological. And, we believe, the converse is also true. Cannot phenomenology be rescued from the taint of subjectivism? In addition, this approach should eliminate dangerous half-truths based on a priori oversimplification. For example, it would be very easy, deductively, to identify the teacher with efficient causation and the student only with the material cause. But the student is not just a block of marble to be "shaped." One of the most important tasks of the teacher is to help the student become his own efficient cause.

There is not much difficulty in identifying knowledge with formal, and the purpose of teaching with final, causation. Since "the means *by which* the teaching activity takes place" is a large, complicated, and extensive topic, we have selected for consideration in Chapter 5 one efficient cause among others, that of the curriculum.[3]

---

[3] A shorter version of this first chapter was presented at the meetings of the American Catholic Philosophical Association in New Orleans, April, 1968, and is published in the *Proceedings* of the Society of the same year.

2

IMMEDIATE AND REMOTE ENDS IN TEACHING AND LEARNING

Since teaching is a human activity and not merely a "relation," it cannot be understood without considering the four factors (K,S,M,E) in their relations with each other. There must be a purpose (E) *for which* the teacher's activity takes place. There must be some means (M) *by which* it takes place. Some kind of knowledge (K) is *what* is taught and, finally, there must be someone (S) *who* is taught. That there are these four, and only four causes is simply a fact discovered by analysis. One may theorize about this fact, but it is not itself something deduced from a theory. It is necessary to mention this only because in the minds of some the names of the four causes and their historical associations, going back to Aristotle, may produce unfavorable emotional overtones. The Who, What, How and Why of teaching correspond, respectively, to what have been called the material, formal, efficient, and final causes. There would seem to be no reason to invent new names to replace the old ones. What is required is an understanding of the role each kind of cause plays in the activity of teaching. It can be said that the teacher causes knowledge in the student, but it should be evident that such a statement requires some analysis.

We shall speak indifferently of the end or purpose of teaching, unless there is some good reason to make a distinction. However, a distinction must be made between immediate and remote ends. There is one immediate end of teaching: to eliminate ignorance of a certain kind in the student, or to cause knowledge of a certain kind in the student. This may be said to be the purpose for which teaching exists. This immediate end is also the first purpose of learning; or, more exactly, of trying to learn, for in fact learning *is* the liquidation of ignorance. The problem of whether teaching ought to be defined and analyzed descriptively or normatively is not relevant at this point, and in saying this I do not believe any "category mistake" is being made. In so far as a student tries to learn and is successful, then his purpose is accomplished and the learning becomes a fact. Also, in so far as the teacher tries to teach, and is successful, then his purpose is accomplished and he *in fact* teaches and the student *in fact* learns—at least to some degree. The activity of teaching cannot be understood thoroughly without considering the purpose for which the activity exists.

The question may be raised: If a student can learn without a teacher, why is it not possible for a teacher to teach without a student learning? Why not define learning and teaching descriptively, each in abstraction from the other? To answer this we may, in the first place, recall that what the student learns without a teacher, present or remote (e.g., a book) is very little and, in any case, is of slight relevance to the problem of teaching and learning in a school. Secondly, if the essence of teaching is defined in complete abstraction from learning, then the relation of the one to the other would be purely accidental. Thirdly, when a student learns, the purpose, i.e., the elimination of ignorance, is the same as the activity of learning itself. But when a teacher teaches, the purpose of the teaching is not teaching itself. The activity of teaching is not the same as the purpose of teaching. Rather, the purpose of teaching is to cause the learning of the student. A teacher may indulge in a great deal of talking and other kinds of physical and mental activity. But if, literally, a student never learns anything of the subject matter, then it is difficult to understand how the teacher may be said to have taught, however good his intentions or however hard he tried. Parenthetically, it may be noted that in such a case the fact does not alone determine the locus of responsibility.

There is still an ambiguity lurking in the phrases "elimination of ignorance" and "causing knowledge in the student." The question may be asked: Must the knowledge the teacher teaches be the same kind as the knowledge the student learns? It would seem that an affirmative answer is necessary. The question is phrased in terms of "must," not "is," because the problem is that of the essential nature of teaching and not merely accidental happenings. If a teacher in an institution has as his purpose the teaching of a certain kind of knowledge (K), it may be, and frequently is in fact, the case that the student learns in addition something else, say, K_2, as well as other miscellaneous bits of knowledge. One reason among others for this is that a curriculum in a school may be, in certain respects, much broader and more inclusive than is the specific kind of knowledge for which the curriculum serves as a means. And yet, what the teacher aims to teach and what the student learns cannot be totally different. If there were not some sameness in the kind of knowledge caused by the teacher in the student, and hence learned by the student, then there could not be teaching. The activity that goes on would have to be called by another name. Even the school could not be called a "school."

In saying this, rather bluntly and briefly, we are quite aware of the fact that there are some philosophers of education who may not agree, at least in appearance, e.g., M. J. Aschner. Yet the thesis here presented would seem to be compatible with the conclusions arrived at through linguistic analysis by such philosophers as Gilbert Ryle—with his distinction between "achievement verbs" and "process verbs"—Israel Scheffler, B. Othanel Smith, and D. B. Gowin.[1] Resolution of the debate might be possible in terms of the distinction we have made, between total and partial success in teaching.

There is a difference between what might be called the "logic" of the learning activity, and the "psychology" of learning. We have been concerned with the logical necessity of learning and teaching, not with what either teacher or student may be conscious of. Of course, it may be said that both should have as a conscious purpose that which is logically demanded by their activities, and in the absence of which their activities would be relatively ineffective, perverted, or even meaningless. This ideal convergence of logical and psychological is partly a function of the maturity of the student. On the higher levels of education, the student is more likely consciously to want to get to know that which the teacher is trying to teach him, that which is necessary for him to know in the light of his more remote ends. If a student aims at becoming an engineer, the knowledge of mathematics is necessary. It is unlikely that he will not want to know mathematics, not want to eliminate his ignorance. He sees the logical relation, which is a relation in the order of knowledge, and understands to some extent the necessity of conforming to it if his remote end, being an engineer, is to be achieved.

The matter is somewhat different when one considers the lower levels of education. There the gap between the psychological and

[1] D. B. Gowin, "Teaching, Learning and Thirdness," *Studies in Philosophy and Education*, Aug., 1961.

For a Critique of Prof. Gowin, see M. J. Aschner, "Teaching, Learning and Mr. Gowin," *Studies in Philosophy and Education*, Spring, 1962, p. 172 ff.

Gilbert Ryle, *The Concept of Mind*, London: Hutchinson House, 1949, pp. 130, 150–151.

Israel Scheffler, *The Language of Education*, Springfield, Ill.; Charles C Thomas, 1960; also, *Conditions of Knowledge*, Glenview, Ill.; Scott, Foresman and Co., 1965.

B. Othanel Smith, "A Concept of Teaching," *Language and Concepts in Education*, (eds.) B. Othanel Smith and Robert H. Ennis, Chicago; Rand McNally and Co., 1961.

the logical is greater. It would not only be "news" to the six- or seven-year-old student, but naivete on the part of adults, to assume that he, the student, consciously wants to "get to know," to eliminate ignorance in certain respects. He may so want, in a sort of subconscious or nonconscious way. It is more likely that what he is conscious of in being at school is that he is there because his parents sent him. The educational purpose may be relatively clear in the minds of both parents and teachers, but certainly not in the same sense—if in fact, in any sense—in the mind of the student. It is for this reason that in schooling it is so important that the nature of the kind of knowledge taught, and the same learned by the student, should not be abstracted from the purposes for which it is taught and learned. In short, one kind of knowledge the student should gradually be introduced to as the educational years proceed, *is the purpose of schooling itself, its value and importance to the student for both his immediate and remote ends.* To the extent that this is properly done by an institution, then the gap, and hence the possibility of conflict, between the logical and the psychological is eliminated.

In addition to the immediate end, *which must be the same for teacher and student*, if the teaching and the learning are to be effective, there are also the more remote ends or purposes. Now the question may be raised: Is it necessary, in order that teaching be effective, that the teacher and the student have the same remote ends? Or, may they differ?

In answering this question, a confusion of modalities must be avoided. One cannot argue that ideally they ought to be the same, and hence they are the same. Nor is the converse argument permissible. But, on the other hand, neither can it be argued that because the remote ends of the teacher and student *may* differ, that therefore they should or *must* differ.

Experientially, and hence a matter of fact, it would seem that the correct answer is that although the immediate aim of teacher and student must be the same in order to make teaching possible, the remote aims may be quite different. A student is studying mathematics. His immediate end is to eliminate his ignorance and get to know mathematics. The immediate aim of the teacher is the same, to help the student do so. But it would seem to make sense to say that the remote end for the student is to get an engineering degree in order that he may make a "living," in order that he may live well, in order that . . . . ; and for the teacher, he teaches in order to make a living, in order that he may live well, in order that . . . . In this case the ends are similar. But equally it may be the case that the student says that he is studying engineering because his father insisted on it, and that when he becomes twenty-one years of age and can legally make his own decisions he will switch to medicine, to which he really wants to devote his vocational efforts. Likewise, the teacher who is teaching mathematics to the student may say that his remote end is to acquire sufficient funds that he may go to engineering college to become an engineer. In this second case, the remote ends of the teacher and the student are in some respects similar and in some respects different.

Now, in both of these hypothetical cases it would seem safe to say that the difference in remote ends on the part of the teacher and the student makes no difference to the immediate end. In any case, regardless of the reasons why, the teacher causes knowledge in the student, and the student learns and gets to know mathematics to a certain extent. In short, it would seem that the remote ends for both teacher and student may be different, and hence apparently irrelevant to the common immediate end of both.

Yet, appearances may be deceiving. Or, perhaps, they are not the whole story. The conclusion arrived at may give one an uneasy feeling. An immediate end stands as a means to the more remote ends in a hierarchy of means-ends relationships, or of values. How, then, can an immediate end be irrelevant to more remote ends? The obvious answer is that an immediate end can function as the same means to the different remote ends held by the teacher and student. In general, this seems to be true. But, again, perhaps it is not the whole truth. Let us reexamine the problem by being more specific.

Both Peter and Paul are in grade eleven, taking a course in mathematics. Peter has also a vocational purpose in mind, for he wants to become an engineer. And he wants to get through school as soon as possible in order to get a job, earn money, get married, and raise a family. A motivational reinforcement is added by the fact that his father's savings will be used to help finance his engineering education. Paul's more remote end is simply getting a "liberal" education. Getting to know mathematics has not only an intrinsic value, but is also a necessary, though not sufficient, means for "understanding the world" in which he lives. Vocational ends are somewhat unclear to him as yet. He has started to read the philosophers, encouraged to do so by his parents, and he has the hope of someday becoming a literary critic. Now again, it may be asked: Cannot each learn the Binomial Theorem, that two plus two equals four, and so on, even though the remote ends of Peter and Paul, and those of the teacher, are completely irrelevant?

If it seems so, then it is because there is a blurring over of the distinction between two orders, the order of knowledge and the order of teaching and learning. An example may illustrate.

It so happens that there is trouble in the school. The teacher, Mr. Smith, is teaching what has recently been called in the United States the "new mathematics." He introduces into his course "strange" notions such as "sets." He talks about the method and logic of mathematics, and its philosophical foundations. Paul is enjoying the course. Peter believes that the teacher is wasting his (Peter's) time, that such "stuff" cannot be used later in engineering, and hence has no practical value. His parents agree, and together they protest to the authorities of the school, for Peter has lost interest in the course and is not learning or getting to know mathematics *as taught by* Mr. Smith. Here, clearly, would seem to be an example of different remote ends on the part of teacher and student affecting achievement of the immediate aim. However, the conflict arises not so much from the conception of mathematics as a kind of knowledge, as from mathematics conceived of as a curriculum category on the level of the order of teaching and learning. The following analysis may demonstrate this, and also may finally allow some general principle to emerge relative to immediate and remote ends in the teacher-student relationship. First, however, we may refer to an important distinction.

Reference has already been made to Mr. Alburey Castell's distinction of two senses of the word "learn." We shall make use of this distinction in our analysis, and its understanding is of such importance as perhaps to justify some long quotations. Mr. Castell says:

In sense I, "getting to parrot," you can learn what is meaningful but false, e.g., that 2 + 2 = 5; or that the earth is shaped like a cube. You can also learn what is meaningful even though you do not know what it means; e.g. "Felix qui potuit rerum cognoscere causas" when you know no Latin. You can also learn what is meaningless; e.g. "Twas brillig and the slithey toves did gyre and gimble in the wabe." You can also learn what is meaningful and true, in your own language, even though you do not understand it; e.g. "Axiology includes ethics and esthetics but not logic." You can also learn what is meaningful and true, in your own language, even though you do understand it; e.g. "Shakespeare is the author of *Hamlet*." In this first sense of "learn," you can learn while you are asleep or while you are under hypnosis. Indeed, so long as you have acquired, retained, and are able to reproduce or repeat, you can be said to have learned in sense I. Learn, in this sense of getting to parrot, covers a lot of territory.

In this sense of getting to parrot, learning . . . has no essential reference to true or false, probable or improbable, rational or irrational, consistent or inconsistent, meaningful or meaningless, understood or not understood. It is not subject to any of the modes of criticism or constraint that apply to learning in sense II, "getting to know."

In sense II, "getting to know," you can learn that 2 + 2 = 4, or that the earth is shaped like an oblate spheroid; but you cannot learn that 2 + 2 = 5, or that the earth is shaped like a cube. To put the point in general terms: in sense II you can learn what is so; but you cannot learn what is not so. If something is meaningless, you cannot learn it, in sense II. If something is meaningful but you do not know what it means, then you cannot learn it in sense II until you do get to know what it means. [Learning in sense II] has essential reference to true and false, probable and improbable, rational and irrational, consistent and inconsistent, meaningful and meaningless, understood and not understood. It is subject to modes of criticism and constraint, arising out of its objectivity, that do not apply to learning in sense I, getting to parrot. To acquire, retain and reproduce or repeat, while sufficient as an account of learning in sense I, will not suffice as an account of learning in sense II. If, in sense II, a person says he learned that 2 + 2 = 5, or that the earth is shaped like a cube, you do *not* concede his point and let him alone. If, still in sense II, he says that he intends to learn these things, you may indeed acknowledge his intention, but you point out that in attempting to carry it out he will encounter frustration. When you say "learn" in sense II, you are not free to say "What I have learned, I have learned," and hope to let it go at that; qua learner, in sense II, you are not immune to criticism.[2]

[2] Alburey Castell, "Two Senses of 'Learn,'" *Oregon Higher Education*, June, 1963, pp. 1, 2.

The sharpness of the distinction of the two senses of "learn" is undoubtedly not to be found in the learning of any student. Perhaps there is always a little of each, and education at its best aims to lead the student from learning, sense I, to learning, sense II. A minor criticism may be made of Mr. Castell's distinction, to be made use of later. Although the quotations do not do justice to the whole article, nevertheless I believe that there are really three senses of the word "learn"—(1) getting to parrot; (2) getting to know *that*; (3) getting to know *why*. The latter two are really distinctions within Mr. Castell's meaning of learning, sense II.

Mr. Castell quite correctly points out that the two senses of "learn" also require two senses of "teach." "Pedagogy, sense I, aims to initiate and sustain in the mind of the beneficiary those activities which bring about, or enable him to bring about learning in sense I. Pedagogy, sense II, aims similarly to bring about learning in sense II."[3] If the additional distinction we have made is admitted, then we can also speak of teaching or pedagogy in sense III.

If so, then we may now understand that the teacher, Mr. Smith, is trying to get Peter to know, to learn in sense III, and not merely in senses I and II. Peter, not understanding the whole situation, wants to stop at learning in sense I or II. The cause of the trouble lies in the differing remote ends of teacher and student.

But there is more to the story. Peter and his parents do not understand the differences between mathematics as a kind of knowledge, and mathematics as a curriculum category in the order of teaching and learning. In studying mathematics, certain rational methods will be used, and the teacher wants Peter to understand them. Hence, in addition to the study of mathematical quantities, the teacher, Mr. Smith, expounds on the nature of the method in mathematics, its "logic," and perhaps the "philosophical founddation" of mathematics.

Now, when one uses logical methods in studying quantities, one is not studying logic. But, if one studies the methods used, then there is a change in formal subject matter (for the "formal object" has changed); and now the kind of knowledge to be learned is not

[3] *Ibid.*, pp. 6, 7.

mathematics, but rather some aspects of the kind of knowledge called "logic." Mr. Smith is not only teaching mathematics, but also a "course" in mathematics. The word "mathematics" refers to two different concepts—mathematics as a kind of knowledge, and as a course in a curriculum. Mathematics as a "course" actually includes two kinds of knowledge, mathematics and logic.

Whether it is best to have the student get to know some logic in this manner, or learn it in a separate course, is another matter, and at present is not the issue. The point is that Mr. Smith is trying to get Peter to know *why* in mathematics, and not merely to know *that*. What is "new" in the "new mathematics" is not the mathematics. Rather, it is the additional elements in the course, the logic and the philosophy. Also, it is this which is the difference between teaching a course in mathematics in a purely vocational curriculum and in a liberal curriculum. The difference is not in the mathematics. Mathematics as a kind of knowledge remains just what it is, and is the same in both cases. It is not the function of pedagogy to change the nature of a kind of knowledge. Its function is to help the student learn; and in the case at hand, Mr. Smith is so trying by using one kind of knowledge, logic, to help Peter understand another kind of knowledge, mathematics.

It is to be noted that this pedagogical instrumentality of logic to mathematics also works the other way around. In a course in logic the teacher may use mathematics to illustrate, not the whole of logic, but a part of its total subject matter. But this instrumentality holds only in the order of teaching and learning, not at all in the order of knowledge. In the order of knowledge, the different kinds of knowledge are related to each other in the ways of evidence, that which bears on truth. In this order, neither logic nor mathematics is instrumental to the other. A proposition of logic cannot be evidence for the truth of a proposition of mathematics; nor conversely.

Before proceeding further we may summarize by stating the following conclusions. Difference in remote ends between a teacher and a student may cause both teaching and learning to be relatively ineffective. Identity in remote ends is not required, but some minimal agreement is. Furthermore it is not difference per se that causes the trouble. Rather, it is the kind of difference that results in incompatibility. What is required for effective teaching and learning is that the different hierarchies of means, i.e., the ends for teacher and student be not incompatible with the immediate end which they have in common, the learning of the student.

What can be done to eliminate the conflict in remote ends that makes for ineffective teaching and learning? Certainly no new pedagogical tricks can do it, for the problem transcends that level. It may be suggested that the teacher change the course to a more vocational nature, thus satisfying Peter and his parents. Of course, this is hardly an answer. Rather, it would be a desperate expedient taken in the absence of an answer. In the first place, in so placating Peter the problem has simply been shifted to a conflict between the remote ends of Paul and the teacher. Secondly, the nature of the course in mathematics that the school should have still remains unanswered.

Another suggestion might be to leave the matter of the nature of the course to be determined by a vote of the students. It would also give the students an exercise in the method of "democratic consensus" as a way of solving value-conflicts. Now, this is not the place to deal with the question of "consensus"; it will be dealt with later. But not all matters of value can be solved by voting. There is a great deal of difference between asking students where they would like to go on a picnic, and asking them what a course in mathematics ought to be. The problem at issue is not the "why" of mathematics, but the "why" of the course, and this is a curricular matter having to do with the philosophy of education. Peter and others like him in the class are having difficulty in *getting to know* the "why" of mathematics. There is little reason to assume that they *already* know the philosophical issues involved in the "why" of the course. In fact, even this is an understatement. Students like Peter are having their difficulties precisely *because* they lack understanding of the philosophical issues. And on these matters voting would merely express, not eliminate, their ignorance.

The school must have a minimal corporate unity, so far as educational purpose is concerned. Otherwise, there would be chaos. It may be granted, in fact insisted upon, that a school neither can nor should not—and not even the parents—determine for Peter his specific vocation. However, the issue at hand is one of educational philosophy, and on that matter the school should have the responsibility and authority correlative with its power.

Finally—and here we are trying to exhaust all alternatives—it is no answer to have Peter change to some other school. The problem still remains. Peter, as one student among others, has simply managed to avoid it. We suggest that all this is true even though, in some given case, it might be wise for a student to change schools, or even to become a "drop-out." However, in this hypothetical case Peter is a "type," and we must proceed on that basis.

Clearly, there is something that should be explained to Peter and his parents. Three questions may be asked. *What* is it that Peter needs to know? *Who* is to inform him? And, *how* is this to be done?

In order that Peter may be helped, what is it that Peter (and others like him) needs to know? Perhaps his teacher, Mr. Smith, should tell Peter that he (Smith) knows better than the student how a course in mathematics should be taught, that he has studied such matters for some years, having obtained a master's degree in his subject, that if a student is to learn he must have humility and faith in the teacher, and that he should accept and not rebel against legitimate authority.

This is an answer of a kind. It may "work." Let us even grant that what the teacher says is true. The trouble is that it is not satisfactory because it is not sufficient. Furthermore, there is a contradiction of sorts. Making use of the distinctions we have made before, the teacher is trying to get Peter to learn the "why" of mathematics, which is learning, sense III. Peter is satisfied with learning, sense II (or I according to Castell), simply knowing the *that* in mathematics. Now, what Mr. Smith is doing in giving the above answer to Peter is "telling" him in sense II (according to Castell, sense I). The teacher only tells Peter *that* he should understand the "why" of mathematics. What should be explained to Peter is the "why" of the *course*—*why* one should understand the "why," not merely the "that," of mathematics. How can one teach "liberally" a course in mathematics (which requires the "why" of mathematics), and at the same time not explain to the student *why* the "why" of mathematics is important to know?

A critic may point out that, if this be so, then the implications of this conclusion are rather startling. For what we are saying is that, if any course is to be taught "liberally," then it is necessary, not merely desirable, that the student also be taught philosophy. If he is to get a liberal and not merely a vocational education, he should understand why, he must come to grips with the philosophical foundations of the subjects he studies. This may require a course in philosophy, if and whenever, courses are taught "liberally"; and, if not a course, then at least teachers who can explain to students the philosophical "why" of the specific subject matter they are teaching.

Now, the critic is quite correct; in fact he is not a critic at all. What he considers "startling" is *only* so relative to present practice in Western civilization. All of which means that perhaps there should be more of a correspondence between theory and practice, and that we can no longer afford the gap—which is responsible for many of the problems faced in education, not only in the so-called "West," but throughout the world.

In saying that Peter needs to know philosophy in order to resolve the conflict of remote ends that renders his learning ineffective, it should be noted that philosophy is required on two different levels: the philosophical foundation of mathematics and the philosophy of education which justifies the course. From the standpoint of causality, Peter lacks understanding of the philosophical foundations of mathematics *because* he lacks understanding of the philosophical justification of the course.

Is there any way of avoiding these conclusions? There is a certain necessity about them, a necessity that is not purely formal. We mention this because a certain type of criticism could be raised at this point that is somewhat irrelevant. Let us suppose that someone says that the kind of necessity we have demonstrated is of a purely formal kind. That is, granting our presuppositions our conclusions follow. However, on other presuppositions contrary conclusions may follow. Of course, this may be granted. But it lacks relevance because the argument does not come to grips with what *is* relevant, the question of the truth or falsity of the presuppositions. A train of reasoning may have a formal necessity, whether or not the premises and conclusions are true or false. However, the conclusions have a substantial or material, and not merely a formal, necessity about them if they are true because one must accept the truth of the premises. If our presuppositions were purely arbitrary, mere "posits," then the matter would be different. Whatever order there may be on the level of teaching and learning is something to be discovered and described, and is not merely a formal order or a mental construction to be imposed on teaching and learning activities.

What are the presuppositions? And can their truth be denied? We have accepted the proposition that it is good to learn, to get to know, to eliminate ignorance. We have accepted the proposition that it is better to know "why" than to remain satisfied with merely knowing "that." Is this an arbitrary value judgment? No. Its truth rests upon the *fact* that although one can in a sense know "that" without knowing "why," the converse does not hold, and hence knowing "why" makes for a fuller and more complete understanding. Any "postulates" denying these truths would be false. Undoubtedly, one can deduce that a philosophical understanding is not necessary for Peter. The reasoning may be formally consistent, but the conclusion would be false because what is postulated is false.

What "liberates" one from ignorance is the more complete, not the less, understanding. It is in this minimal, not exhaustive, sense that we have spoken of "liberal education" rather than vocational education. The emphasis is not on the "when" of such education. In the example given, it was grade eleven. It might have been some other grade. In most countries in the world there is a rough division between primary, secondary, and higher education, however it may be broken up and under whatever different names. Some systems and divisions may be better that others. The term "grade" has been used to avoid referring to any system of any country. Certainly, somewhere between grades 11 and 13 is to be found liberal education, if it is to be found at all.

We would not want to imply that there must be an absolute break between nonliberal, liberal, and professional education. Rather, it is a matter of emphasis. In terms of the three senses of "learning," it seems safe to say that all three senses are to be found to some extent on all levels of education. It is a matter of degree. The lower the grade the more learnings in senses I and II predominate. The higher the grade the more sense III should predominate, although often in practice such a neat correlation may not be found.

This correlation, however "rough" it may be found to be in reality, has a certain necessity about it because it is based not merely on human ideality but on human nature. The student must of necessity do a lot of "getting to know *that*," before he can be very efficacious on the level of "getting to know *why*." In the lower grades the student should learn to calculate, not primarily to philosophize about mathematics. Likewise, unless he acquires a great deal of information on what are called "historical facts," he will later not have anything to philosophize about when he comes to the "philosophy of history."

It needs to be said again that the order of priority is one of emphasis only. A stronger thesis would go beyond what the evidence allows. There is no reason to believe that liberal education can only begin at a certain age, and that in all the prior years the education must be one hundred percent nonliberal.

What happens if this order of priority is denied in practice? The student grows up lacking in informational knowledge in mathematics, history, and other subjects. Since this cannot be justified on philosophical grounds, then philosophical truth could hardly have been taught to the student. What was it, then? The student would have to be indoctrinated in some kind of ideology. An ideology does not have to be true or false, only useful for some purpose. Hence, the aim in the courses is not so much that of getting to know mathematics and history; rather, these names now refer to curricular entities which are instrumental to (say) getting the student to "adjust to his environment," or.... It is this that explains in part the reason for the criticism of recent educational theories and practices as given by a group such as the Council for Basic Education.

If it is certain that Peter needs to know philosophy in order to be most effective in his learning, then two other questions arise: who should teach him and how should it be done? Here we are dealing with alternative means. Can the answers be so clear? The answer to the first question was on the level of principle, and was arrived at by understanding what is intrinsic to the teaching and learning activities. But the questions of "who" and "how" are on the level of means, and it is in the very nature of a means to be related to some concrete existential set of circumstances *to which* it is a means. In short, the choice of a means cannot alone be determined rationally by deducing it from a principle. This would seem to render rather hopeless the attempt to answer these questions in abstraction from some specific situation.

However, the task is not at all hopeless if we refer to general rather than specific means, and that is really what the problem is about. Let us consider for a moment this distinction. One can speak generally and say that eating food is a means—in this case, a *necessary* means—to health for any human being. As regards evidence, all that is required is knowledge of the essential nature of the human being. Of course, there is no *existential* human nature in general. Only Peter, Paul, John, etc., exist in a given time and place under specific conditions. Yet, such specificity is irrelevant as evidence to the proposition stating means, "generally." Without knowing John, we can nevertheless say that food is a means to his health. However, we cannot argue that since cabbage is a food, therefore cabbage is good for John. It may or may not be. John might have an "allergy." And so we can say that John as a human being needs to know philosophy, and that it should be taught to him, at the same time granting that some particular John—and not John as a "type"—may for some good reason be an exception. It may be that this particular John Jones has already, by the 11th grade, been "educated beyond his capacity," that perhaps he should change either his school or curriculum and go into some kind of vocational program of studies. But even if this be the case with respect to a specific means for John, the problem of the general means still remains for others who can profit by something more than a purely vocational approach to schooling.

Returning to Peter, he may be taught philosophy in either one of two ways by his teacher, Mr. Smith—in the activity of teaching mathematics or in a separate course in philosophy as part of the curriculum. Another alternative would be a combination of both. In considering the alternatives we shall be seeking the *necessary* requirements for effective teaching of philosophy. Let us consider the case in which Mr. Smith teaches Peter philosophy in his course in mathematics.

1. Except as a happy accident the teacher cannot cause knowledge of a certain kind in a student unless the teacher himself knows that kind of knowledge. He cannot teach sense II unless he has already learned sense II. As Mr. Castell puts it:

> First, you must know, possess as learning sense II, what you propose to teach; and what is more, you must know that you know this. This is essential. You must yourself have experienced what it means to have done some learning, in sense II. It is through reflecting on such experience that you get to know that you know. Without this, you do not know what you are trying to bring about, or facilitate, in the mind of the beneficiary. You must know, from your own experience, what it is to discover or show that what you claim to learn, sense II, is required, necessitated, by what you already know.
> Second, you must know the mind, or the content of the mind, of the beneficiary. This is essential. You must know what it is that he knows and how he knows it. In these matters he must not be a "stranger" to you. The reason is that you propose to add something which will be entailed by what he already knows. You propose to teach him X, in sense II. When you are finished he will *know* X. To do this you must know whether what he already knows requires, necessitates, what you propose to teach him in sense II. If it does not, then you cannot teach him, in sense II, what you propose to teach him. You can "tell" him, but that would only be pedagogy sense I, and (except by happy accident) will not bring about learning in sense II. It is as necessary for you to know, learn, the mind of the beneficiary as it is for you to know, learn, what you would add to his present knowledge. To the degree that you do not meet this second condition, he will have to use what you teach him (in sense I) to teach himself in sense II. What is sometimes called "knowing your stuff," i.e., your subject, is necessary but not sufficient. You must also know, and know how to get to know, and know how to make a required addition to the mind of the beneficiary. Pedagogy in sense II is difficult business; how difficult can perhaps be appreciated only by those who, knowing what they are trying to do, try and fail.[4]

It is as simple as this: Mr. Smith cannot teach the "why" of mathematics unless he has already learned it. The simplicity of this truth is not at all changed by the fact that, as any experienced teacher knows, in the act of teaching one's learning of the subject

---
[4] *Ibid.*, p. 8.

is increased—thus giving rise to the old witticism that the best way to learn a subject is to teach it. Needless to say, one's learning through teaching is increased only because one first learned something that could be increased.

How much philosophy does the teacher need to know? Of course, ideally, the more the better. But our answer must be in terms of necessity, not ideality. The teacher must know as much philosophy as is required for the student to learn "why" of mathematics at the given level on which he is a student. As the level changes, the "amount" to be known changes. In teaching Peter the logic and philosophical foundations of mathematics, Mr. Smith does not have to be a professional philosopher or logician. It would be a kind of professional sin of pride on the part of the philosopher to demand it. Neither the amount of, nor depth in, philosophy would be required in the early-grade courses in mathematics that would be required of a teacher in a graduate school of mathematics.

2. Another requirement is that the teacher separate for the student, by careful distinctions, the two different formal subject-matters. Let us recall, again, that when a teacher teaches the student to reason correctly in mathematics, the teacher is teaching mathematics and not logic. However, if there is a change in the formal object of study, and now there is not the use of the method but rather a reflective analysis on the method used, then, whether the teacher knows it or not, and for better or worse, he is teaching some logic. A denial of this distinction, because of a lack of knowledge on the part of the teacher, will probably find its effect in the learning of the student.

Although a teacher can cause learning in a student, he cannot cause ignorance in the student, for the ignorance is already there, a given fact. However, unfortunately, any serious lack of knowledge on the part of the teacher may intensify the ignorance of the student, and make it all the more difficult for him to learn.

To illustrate, let us suppose that, through ignorance, bad faith, or both, the teacher falls into the vice of "academic imperialism" and reduces another kind of knowledge to the one he is teaching. In the case at hand he would implicitly or explicitly tend to identify logic and mathematics. The student in later years may never study logic systematically in a course, for hasn't he already had it? Not understanding that even formal logic is not identical with mathematics, although mathematical reasoning will be formally logical, and not understanding that there are other logical methods because there are other formal subject matters, the student may go through life self-righteously congratulating himself on his rigorous thinking, and directly or indirectly condemning or feeling sorry for his colleagues who do not think so clearly. Or, he may get creative in a "philosophical" way and try to show how other kinds of knowledge can be, and ought to be, understood in terms of mathematical models.

To the perceptive reader the generality of our illustrations will not hide the fact that what we have analyzed is not something purely hypothetical, but is actually descriptive of much so-called education, past and current. For what a mathematics teacher can do, other teachers can also do.

3. In the process of distinguishing between the two subject matters, mathematics and philosophy, the teacher should define, hence delimit, the nature of each subject. Obviously, the degree to which this is done will depend upon the grade-level of the student. But it must be done. Whatever is or is not done by the teacher, the student will have some idea—true, false, hazy, etc.—of *what* mathematics is. There is no alternative here. The alternatives lie only in whether he knows relatively well or not.

Nor is there any alternative, from the standpoint of the teacher, as to whether or not he makes statements about the subject matter he teaches. It is impossible to teach mathematics (in contrast to doing mathematics) without saying something about it. But when one says something about mathematics, one is not talking mathematics, for there is a difference between propositions *of* and propositions *about* any given kind of knowledge. A proposition *about* what mathematics is is not itself a mathematical proposition. Rather, it is a proposition on the level of the order of knowledge, a part of the theory of knowledge, which is part of philosophy. If the teacher says that mathematics is an important kind of knowledge to know, then he is evaluating mathematics. If he says that calculus was discovered by Newton and Leibnitz, then he is saying something about the history of mathematics. Historical propositions are not propositions *of*, but may be *about*, mathematics. That is, they do not enter into mathematical operations in the way of evidence or proof in the *doing* of mathematics. They are, however, not merely relevant but also necessary in the teaching of mathematics, that is, to mathematics as a curriculum, not a knowledge, category.

Thus far we have considered only what the teacher must know philosophically in helping the student to get to know the "why" of mathematics. There still remains the philosophical problem of explaining the "why" of the course. For, let us recall, in the order of causality it was a lack of understanding that prevented Peter from properly liquidating his ignorance and getting to know the "why" of mathematics. Now, this problem of the "why" of this course is a curricular problem at least, and such a problem is in part a problem of the philosophy of education. It will not be necessary, here, to explain exactly what the philosophy of education is. As a subject it is perhaps more practical than theoretical; but in any case it either is, or presupposes, philosophy theoretically.

And now, what are the necessary requirements which must be satisfied if the teacher is to explain, and the student is to learn, the "why" of the course?

1. The teacher should know, in some minimal sense surely, the philosophy of education. Without belaboring the obvious, this is in accordance with the principle that a teacher cannot cause the learning of a subject by the student, that is, cannot teach the subject, unless he knows it. Since perfect knowledge does not exist, and is only approximated, the degree to which this requirement will be necessary depends in part, if not wholly, on the grade level the teacher is teaching.

2. The teacher should know the meaning of a curriculum, the difference between a "knowledge category" and a "curriculum category," and know that what constitutes the one is not identical with what constitutes the other.

3. He should know something about the meaning of a liberal education in contrast to a merely vocational one. This will require some knowledge of the relation of the ends of liberal education to other important ends and purposes in human living. Specifically, he should know what fundamental kinds of knowledge there are,

what constitutes them as knowledge, and the different methods of discovering different modes of truth. He will then be better able to explain the nature, and the "why," of the special subject he is teaching. In the degree to which he is successful, the student will learn the "why" of the course, thus enabling him, both motivationally and intellectually, to learn the "why" of the kind of knowledge he is studying.

4. On all of these matters there must be some minimal agreement between any one teacher, say Mr. Smith, and other teachers in the school. To the degree this is not attained, then so much the worse for the student and the school. At least in the early grades, and perhaps for some time later, any confusion on these matters on the part of the teachers should be withheld from the students. This is morally justifiable, for it is not knowledge that is being withheld from the student. Rather, it is the lack of knowledge of the teacher that is withheld, or at least held in check.

5. Finally, a most necessary requirement is that Mr. Smith and other teachers like him, have the confidence of the school in explaining to the student the "why" both of the special subject matter and the course. Otherwise, there would be a contradiction, a conflict, between what is done in the classroom teaching and the corporate unity or purpose of the school. This conflict cannot long be hushed up even by the compromises that constitute expediency. It will be only a question of time until the conflict is passed on to the student. He may only be half-conscious of the conflict. But even if he is conscious of it, he will not thoroughly understand it. Nevertheless it will be reflected in him emotionally, creating attitudes that will make it all the more difficult to learn.

If these seem like impossible demands to make upon the activity of teaching, then perhaps there is a misunderstanding. What we have been describing is the order *intrinsic* to the teaching and learning activities. We have not been describing what goes on under the name of teaching and learning in various places and at different times. The truth of such descriptions would vary with time and place. Is, then, this order we have been describing a norm in terms of which teaching and learning activities that take place at given times and places, and under given conditions, may be judged? The answer is, of course, yes.

However, a caveat is in order. The term "norm" is ambiguous. Sometimes norms are spoken of as if they are purely subjective, and undoubtedly there are such. But if all norms are arbitrary, capricious, and subjective, then one is doomed to a doctrinal skepticism—in which case there can be no false answers on the matter of the order of teaching and learning precisely because there can be no true ones. In fact, there is no rational problem at all.

The principles that we have been describing have their foundation "in the nature of things," not in some "ideal posit" of one or more persons. In this case, the "nature of things" refers to the teaching and learning activities, and in particular to the way in which a student "gets to know" something. There are dietetic norms describing what, within the proper limitations, one ought to eat to be healthy. But here the "ought" has a *necessity* about it. One could just as accurately—again, within the proper limitations—speak of what one *must* eat to be healthy. Nothing is changed and, in fact, it would be somewhat irrelevant to point out that such a necessity is only hypothetical and not categorical. "If it is good to be healthy, then one ought or must. . . ."

The presupposition is that it is good to be healthy. But it is not an arbitrary, merely subjective ideal. Of course, a person has the freedom to make an "ideal" out of bad health. He also has the freedom to act on falsehoods. However, what is relevant now is not the fact of freedom, but the question of truth and falsity. If it is false that health is good, then all principles of dietetics become mere formal statements like the rules of games, and would have no relevancy at all to the existential condition of man—his physiological nature.

And so with the principles describing the order of teaching and learning. The assumption is that it is good to learn. If that is false, then there is no problem. But if it is true, then necessities (not merely "maybes") follow as to what a teacher and a student must do in order to teach and learn. One ought to do what must be done if teaching and learning are human goods. And just as one may eat relatively well or badly, such eating being appraised in terms of the principles of dietetics, so one may teach or learn relatively well or badly, such activities being appraised in terms of the principles of the order of teaching and learning.

The two questions that were asked—who is to teach the student philosophy, and how is it to be taught—tend to merge into one question for the purpose of analysis. We have considered the alternative of Mr. Smith teaching it, and he does so by introducing the philosophy necessary into his mathematics course. The other alternative as to the "who" and the "how" is to have one or more separate courses in philosophy given as part of the curriculum. There is reason to believe that the alternatives are not exclusive, and that both are necessary.

One would hardly argue the wisdom of introducing a separate course in philosophy in the very early grades. There is such a thing as over-intellectualizing the curriculum. In those grades students are not usually taught "courses," in the ordinary meaning of the term. And it is not at all clear, even as a hypothetical conception, what a course in philosophy would be, let us say, for students in the first two grades.

However, somewhere along the way, whenever liberal education is consciously stressed, the systematic study of philosophy should begin. And as with any other fundamental subject, if philosophy is to be taught rigorously and systematically, then separate attention will have to be given to it. And this separate attention is usually what is meant by a "course."

Having as it does the mark of the temporal, the problem of "when" in education is always a matter of prudential decision. This does not at all imply arbitrariness, for there is evidence to which an appeal can be made. In the first place, the necessities and norms in education are independent of geography, and because human nature is a constant of sorts and not completely a function of circumstances, the "when" in education is not wholly a variable without limits. Secondly, this truth is reflected in different ways in different countries. Whether it be in England, Germany, France, or the United States, if a liberal education is to be given, it is usually between certain ages of a student's career. We believe that this is generally the case, understanding that there are exceptions, and allowance should be made for the differences in institutional mode and manner of expression.

Before pursuing the question of when liberal education should be introduced, and hence when philosophy should be systematically studied, it may be well first to consider a little more clearly the nature of liberal education in contrast to other kinds. In so doing we shall lean rather heavily on an analysis made by Mr. Alburey Castell, together with some minor modifications and additions of our own.

Mr. Castell points out that there are three great rungs on the educational ladder.[5] On the first rung, in the lower grades, the primary task of the student is to acquire facility in such elementary, though fundamental, activities as reading, writing, translating, calculating, etc. Without these elementary learnings the student is ill-prepared if he leaves school, or even if he continues in school. Such learnings are necessary for further progress.

Education on this first rung Mr. Castell calls "technical," a word derived from the Greek word *techne*, meaning "know-how." One can get to know "how" without getting to know "why." One can learn how to add 2 and 2 to get 4 without knowing the reason why it is 4. And such knowledge can be useful even though the student is left with knowledge for which he does not know the reasons. But it "works." However, a mind so circumscribed is "servile," for it has not achieved the "freedom" that comes from knowing the reasons for what one believes, thinks, and does.

To become aware that one is servile is a necessary condition for desiring to become free. At this point education changes from the technical to the liberal, the second rung. Psychologically, either there is, or there should be, instilled in the student those desires based upon the logical implications of the ends of learning—first, the desire to know a great deal more than one has any immediate "practical" need to know; second, the desire to know it in a certain way, namely, in terms of its justifying reasons. In pursuing such ends the student will acquire a liberal education.

The term "liberal education" is sometimes ambiguous. If so, the unclarity is usually in connection with the word "liberal." To educate a person in respect to anything is simply to eliminate his ignorance with respect to that thing. The various ways in which that is done are constituted by the different modes of knowing, which is an epistemological (not a psychological) matter. The

[5] Alburey Castell, "Liberal Education in High School and College," *Journal of General Education*, July, 1963.

present question is what makes an education liberal. It is not sufficient to say that such an education "liberates" one from ignorance. All education does this. Going beyond etymology, what makes an education liberal is that which liberates one from both narrowness and shallowness. Another way of saying it is that knowledge is increased both quantitatively and qualitatively.

By a quantitative increase in knowledge, reference is not now made to an increased accumulation of facts on the "know-how" or "know-that" level, although this is to be desired. Rather, reference is to an increase in range of studies. One moves gradually from the first to the second rung of the educational ladder when a somewhat systematic study is made of a wide range of subjects such as mathematics, the sciences, foreign languages, history, philosophy, literature, and composition. A mind whose holdings are thus extended is liberated from provincialism and parochialism. In the words of Mr. Castell: "To know your way around in algebra as well as arithmetic, in Latin as well as French, in Greek history as well as American history, in logic as well as grammar, in economics as well as civics, is to overcome narrowness in important ways."[6]

Knowledge of ancient and medieval history, as well as modern, is of special importance. Without such knowledge, it has been said, man is condemned to repeat the errors of the past. Who can be more "creative" than the student (and, unfortunately, often the teacher, too) who confuses an old truth or falsity with some "new" idea—that which is really new, being his recent subjective awareness? And how often is the student's "creativity" directly proportional to his ignorance of the past?

But even an extension in kinds of knowledge is not enough. One must also be liberated from shallowness, liberated in a qualitative sense. A great deal of "knowing that" may have been acquired in many subjects, but there still remains the "why," not only the "why" of a special subject matter, but of other kinds too. Why does one know that he knows, and does not just believe? Why do people act as they do, and as they did in the past? What is the meaning of this "history" one has studied? Is there any order or pattern in it? Here, not just history in a "positive" sense is neces-

[6] *Ibid.*, p. 3.

sary, but also the "philosophy of history." And, if there is to be something more than idle speculation and guesswork, some knowledge of philosophy is necessary. One of the primary functions of philosophy—although by no means the only one—is not so much to extend one's holdings knowledgewise as to increase in depth of understanding the holdings already extended.

To return to the example of mathematics once again, one can learn a great deal about numbers without asking or knowing what a number is, or even what kind of knowledge mathematics is. One can do something called "induction" in connection with the Binomial Theorem without understanding what induction is, or whether it is the same kind of "induction" that the physics teacher speaks of in connection with something called the scientific method. What is a student's knowledge *of* in studying mathematics? Is his knowledge that of numbers? Or, is it about "symbolic marks" that refer to numbers? Or, is it only knowledge of the symbols themselves? Or, is it about apples and/or rosary beads that the student uses numbers to calculate?

The second rung has been completed when the student sees that getting to know must be carried to the point where he is responsible and answerable for what he knows. There is a rationale in knowing. To apprehend this as a general fact, and again to apprehend it in specific cases, is necessary if an education is to be liberal in a qualitative sense.

Needless to say, such work is never really finished. But formal schooling is of necessity limited, and at the same time the student must move on, if at all, to the third rung of the educational ladder.

The third rung is also essentially technical. It is the education that produces the professional and managerial classes—the doctors, dentists, veterinarians, engineers, research scientists, architects, clergymen, judges, lawyers, journalists, school teachers, business executives, governmental officials, military and political leaders, and the like. What distinguishes technical education on this rung from that on the first is that it comes *after* liberal education, and hence ideally should be synthesized with it. The recipient of a professional education can think about his profession in a liberal way. Of course, as Mr. Castell points out, a person may not choose to do this. "He may make of himself a slide-rule mechanic, a pill-pushing physician, a case-bound lawyer, a rote-learning pedagogue, a gossip-mongering journalist or a rule-of-thumb architect. But if he does any of these things, it is in spite of, not because of, liberal education acquired on the second rung."[7]

We have spoken of a synthesis of liberal and technical education. If liberal education helps to make man free, it is technical education that gives man power. No modern or contemporary society could long exist without the professional and managerial classes. And in any society it is these classes which most directly exert power over each and everyone of us. It will always be that way whether one knows it or not, or whether one likes it or not. These are the decision makers, and they rule our lives in more ways than we would like to believe. Are these men liberally educated and free men? They had better be so; otherwise, because of their decisions all of us may gradually lose our liberties. Education as liberal, and as technical or vocational, are different; but there need be no conflict. The difference is in primary, not total, aims. It is not the primary purpose of a technical education to be liberal. Nor is it the primary purpose of a liberal education to produce the professional and managerial classes. But, if the two are wholly separated, then a literally immoral—not just "unideal"—situation would eventuate, for responsibility and power would be isolated each from the other, and the common good would suffer.

In mentioning the "common good" we have pointed up the moral issue. By the term "common good" we refer not, of course, to its frequent ideological meaning, but rather to the ethical meaning. Ideologically the common good is usually considered identical with the aims of, or the outcome of the decisions made by, a power elite, regardless of whether or not they reflect the will of a minority group or a majority consensus. In any case there are no norms to be intellectually discovered and in terms of which one wills. Rather, the common good is *what* is willed, and this is simply the old "might is right" doctrine, whatever be the mode of its expression. Power is not to be judged; rather it is the judge.

Such a notion is not one ethical position among others. Instead it is a form of ethical nihilism. In its ethical meaning the "com-

[7] *Ibid.*, p. 6.

mon good" is a notion subsumed under the more general category of justice, which is a virtue. Through the understanding of justice, and its principles which function as norms, man has a rational guide in the formation of decisions and also objective standards in terms of which power may be judged. Therefore, an important part of a liberal education of the professional and managerial classes should include the philosophical, in particular that which is concerned with the ethical. This is not merely a logical, but also a moral, necessity. To the degree that this synthesis of the technical and the liberal is lacking, those who have ethical knowledge will lack power, and those who have power will lack ethical knowledge.

Those who have power should also be free. The common good will suffer to the degree that liberally educated free men are long ruled by powerful men who are not free. In fact, such would be a recipe for social decadence.

That there are these three rungs of the educational ladder can hardly be denied. Therefore, we can now deal with the question that was raised about the "when" of liberal education. Mr. Castell says: "The answer I would propose is that the first rung extends through the tenth grade; that, for a majority of young men and women, the second rung extends through the last two years of high school and the first two years of college; and that the third rung begins to be felt by the junior year in college and increasingly thereafter."[8] The language used reflects the institutional structure of the United States. It may be best to speak of grades 11 through 14.

There is nothing sacrosanct about the numbers 11 or 14. There could be, and is, some legitimate variation. But, if there is to be liberal education at all, then it has to come somewhere in the middle of the educational ladder. Factually, wherever liberal education is found there is a rough approximation to grades 11 through 14. In the United States, these years overlap—because of historical reasons, among others—with high school and college. In France, the termination is with the Lycée, in Germany with the Gymnasium or some corresponding Institute. Although there can be

[8] *Ibid.*, p. 7.

some variation in the matter of the specific years, what is absolute and cannot vary is the necessity of a liberal education; and secondly, it must come after elementary education and before, or at least concomitant with, further technical education.

But even if this is true, a misunderstanding may easily arise. A critic might point out that, although in the abstract there is some truth in the distinctions between knowing "how," "that," and "why," a student's life cannot, and should not, be temporally chopped up accordingly. Does not the whole thesis reflect a very old educational fallacy, one which has long been exposed in educational theory, namely, that of confusing logical and temporal priority? Is there not psychological fact as well as logical necessity? Running the scales on the piano may be logically necessary in order later to play "tuneful" music. But, pedagogically may it not be better first to introduce the beginner in piano to a simple tune and later work into the scales and arpeggios? Why cannot elementary education be liberal, and liberal education elementary? And why cannot professional education be liberal; and conversely? When elementary and so-called "liberal education" are fused together, which has been the aim of many twentieth-century educators, are they to be dismissed by accusing them of merely trying to get students to "adjust to their environments"? In fact, that is only a distorted half of the story. The other half is the most important, namely that of teaching the students how to adjust the environment to themselves. That is the difference between being a victim of nature, including their own natures, and, on the other hand, controlling nature for human ends and purposes.

The point made by the critic is well taken, but perhaps rests on a misunderstanding. It is not wholly clear whether or not Mr. Castell leaves himself open to the criticism. If he does, it is perhaps because in short articles he is limited and that some points of clarification are not to be found. Some of these we shall make, believing them to be compatible with the essential truth of his thesis.

It is correct that temporal and logical priorities should not be confused in this respect; a temporal priority does not always necessarily follow, i.e., cannot be deduced, merely from a logical priority. But that very fact also means that the matter of priorities must be left open to some experimental evidence or experimental fact. Hence, sometimes the logically prior can also be the temporally prior; and conversely. Referring to an example we have given, we have pointed out that it is necessary to calculate before knowing the "why" of mathematics, and also that the knowing *that* is logically prior to the knowing *why*. That the two priorities happen to correspond in such a case is not the result of merely formal, a priori reasoning, but rather is rooted in the experiences of teaching and learning.

Furthermore, the sharpness of the distinction between technical and liberal education does not imply that in considering the "when" in education that it must be equally sharp. Perhaps it should not be, and in fact usually it is not. The point we have made, however, is that the sharpness of the distinction must be reflected temporally, in some manner or other, in the way of emphasis. In the elementary grades, the teacher may introduce the "why" as well as the "how" and the "that" in so far as the student is capable of understanding, providing—and this is most important—first, that the emphasis is not there, and secondly that the "why" is not made a substitute through misplaced emphasis for the "how" and the "that."

Liberal education *as a matter of emphasis* occurs later, when there is deliberate, systematic study of what earlier had been incidentally introduced into curricular programs but was not the chief emphasis. Now, all of this is quite compatible with the thesis sometimes advanced that any kind of knowledge can be taught at any grade level, in some manner or other. If this statement is true, then the qualifying phrase "in some manner or other" is necessary. Without it, the proposition would be too ambiguous. What we have tried to do is to show at least the possibility of the "some manner or other."

There is another criticism that might be made of the sharpness of the distinction between the "that" and the "why" of knowing. Do not these distinctions run through all kinds of education and at all levels? If so, they cannot be used to distinguish liberal from technical education. To illustrate how a whole series of continuous "thats" and "whys" run through the technical or voctional, consider the case of the "old-time" carpenter who is asked, when he builds a house with concrete blocks as a foundation, how he knows that the corners are square. He may explain that with string, or some other measuring instrument, he goes out 3 yards in one direction, and 4 yards "up" in the other direction. Then with another piece of string 5 yards long, he makes adjustments so that the ends meet those of the first two strings. Now, he *knows that* he has a square corner. His father taught him that, and he has used the same method all his life. And it always *works*.

But why does it work? He doesn't know, but his son does. The son is in the 9th grade of a purely vocational school, and is learning a trade. He has been studying plane geometry and he can explain why it works by showing that his father, although not knowing it, was applying the Pythagorean theorem. But the theorem, which is a "why" relative to the father's operation, which in turn is a "that," now itself becomes a "that." For it can be asked of this theorem—why?

Now this series of "thats" and "whys" can be pursued up through higher mathematics, perhaps involving even non-Euclidean geometries, as well as through civil engineering. And all of it is on a purely technical level. If this be true, then can the distinction in question be used to differentiate vocational or technical education from liberal?

The answer is that, without further clarification (which unfortunately Mr. Castell does not give), it can't. This does not mean that what has been said thus far is false; rather, it is insufficient. The distinction between "knowing that" and "knowing why" remains, but there are at least three different kinds of "getting to know why." First, there is the *"why,"* which lies wholly within a given kind of knowledge. Second, there is the "why" which pedagogically requires another kind of knowledge, philosophy. Third, there is the "why" which is intrinsic to philosophy itself. We may illustrate by giving examples of each.

1. The "why" and the "that" may lie wholly within one kind of knowledge. Why is it that 2 and 2 are 4? This can be explained by relating the part to the whole, in this case to the whole cardinal number system. Why is it a fact that the earth goes around the sun in an elliptical orbit? Newton's theory may be used to explain this. Again, there is a kind of relation of a part to

a whole, in this case an added verification of Kepler's hypothesis because it (but not only it) is deducible from Newton's theory. Why did Caesar cross the Rubicon? This can be explained by relating it to a wider range of historical facts. It may be noted that a philosophical discipline, as one kind of knowledge among others, has its own "why" in this first sense.

2. There is the "why" that is extrinsic to a given kind of knowledge, but pedagogically intrinsic to a course given in that kind of knowledge. If in answer to a "why" question in mathematics it is necessary to go into an examination or exposition of the method of mathematics, then one has turned to a philosophical discipline, namely, logic. For, let us recall again, although there is, of course, reasoning in mathematics, the nature of the reasoning is not the formal subject matter of mathematics but rather of logic.

In a class in physics, in order to explain this kind of "why" question, one may go into an explanation of the scientific (experimental) method. Again, the "why" is explained in terms of logic, and it can be good pedagogy in terms of *the course in physics*. However, physics as a kind of knowledge and physics as a curriculum category are not the same. The words are the same, but the conceptual reference is quite different. In physics as strictly a kind of knowledge the scientific method is *used*, but never studied. Again, as in the case of mathematics, although there is reasoning in physics, the nature of the reasoning is not the formal subject matter of physics, but rather of logic. Yet, pedagogically, i.e., from the standpoint of physics as a course or as a curricular category, it may be necessary in order to answer a "why" question to bring to bear another kind of knowledge, logic—one of the philosophical disciplines. Logic, however, is extrinsic to physics in this sense; it is not part of physics. Nor is logic a part of mathematics.

3. If there is an integration of two kinds of knowledge, one of which is ontological (a philosophical and/or theological discipline) and the other is not, then we have a "why" in a third sense. The term "ontological" will be used whenever reference is made, *indifferently*, to theology and/or that part of philosophy which is metaphysics.

Let us suppose the question is asked: Why do human beings die? Now there are a series of "whys" on different levels, all of which are relevant as answers. For example, an answer in terms of physiology would be one kind. But, if one pursues the matter far enough, i.e., *deep* enough, then one is led to some kind of ontological answer. Human beings are one kind of finite beings among others. They come into being and pass away. This is part of their nature as *natural* beings, all of which are contingent. This means that it is not part of the essential nature of man to exist necessarily. And so on. Here the explanation is in terms of those most ultimate of all categories, essence, existence, etc., which are metaphysical. The theologican may go one step further and relate death to sin. Of course, if there is no such thing as theological knowledge, then so be it. However, it is not our function at present to prejudice the matter by such an assumption.

Attention is to be called to the fact that the nature of the "why" in this third sense is irrelevant to the truth or falsity of the example we may use to illustrate it. In terms of the ontology of dialectical materialism, there would be a different explanation of why people die. But it is still an ontological explanation. A false ontological proposition is as much an ontological proposition as a true one—just as a false proposition in, say, chemistry is just as much a proposition of chemistry as a true one.

The complete understanding of "why" in this third sense is too large an undertaking at present, hence will be given separate treatment later. For now, only the distinction need be understood.

It is this third meaning of "why" which makes possible some of those disciplines that are called "the philosophy of . . ."—e.g., the philosophy of nature, the philosophy of human nature, the philosophy of history. However, one must not be misled because of similar words. Not everything that is introduced by the words "philosophy of" can make a claim as a kind of knowledge. As we shall see later, the "philosophy of religion" is not a knowledge category at all, but rather is a curricular category. The failure to understand this has produced a great deal of chaos in higher education.

It is the "why" in this third sense that gives *depth* to a liberal education, that eliminates shallowness, and that defines the qualitative uniqueness of education of this kind. Putting aside the theological for the moment, this means that philosophy has not merely an important place in liberal education, but also a unique function. There are those who would deny the possibility of philosophical knowledge, but usually they are not consistent enough to elicit the full implications of such denial. They will draw them out in practice—there is no doubt about that. The results are evident round and about. But usually a theoretical justification of such practice is not given. And of course there is, interestingly enough, a reason for this. A justification would have to be made on philosophical grounds, or at least there would be philosophical presuppositions. In which case there would be an essential contradiction (not merely a psychological one), for they would be presupposing philosophical truth in the act of denying its possibility.

If there is no philosophical knowledge, then there is no "why" in the third sense. If there is no "why" in the third sense, then there can be none in the second sense, for there is no philosophical knowledge to bring to bear on another subject, such as, say mathematics or the physical sciences. Hence, only "why" in the first sense, is left, if even that is now at all possible! In any case, only the technical remains, and that only in the elementary sense of rung one in the education ladder, for there can be no liberal education. Even the technical education of the professional and managerial classes, which comes *after* a liberal education, and should be synthesized with it, is now reduced to the technical in the elementary sense.

In the social order what remains are human *wills* whose interests, individual and/or collective, are absolute. All that remains is to use the "technical" to satisfy those interests, and education now becomes the chief weapon for this collectivistic task. In drawing out these implications—and to see their necessity—all the same *words* are used—"social," "education," "person," etc. Even the spelling is the same—yet the *conceptual* reference is totally different, for such "knowledge" nihilism presupposes voluntarism and totalitarianism in some form or other. Were it not for the obstacles of language, it would be clearer if different words could be used.

Let us return to the question raised previously. In teaching mathematics, as a kind of knowledge, Mr. Smith introduced in his course some philosophy that is relevant to the knowing of the "why" of mathematics. And so do teachers in other courses. Where should the teacher get his knowledge of philosophy? Evidently he should get it in the way he acquires other kinds of knowledge, through *courses* in which a systematic study is made, and this necessarily includes the history of philosophy. Some time during the years of liberal education the student should be required to study philosophy in the same way. This will now require a professional teacher who will deal in a systematic way with the philosophy which the student encountered in the first rung of the education ladder when it was "brought into" other courses of special subject matter.

The necessity of this can only be understood in terms of the alternative. What is it?

Let us suppose it is suggested that the student does not need courses in philosophy, for he can acquire sufficient knowledge through teachers "bringing it in" when teaching their special subject matters. Hence, courses in philosophy, if given at all, should remain elective for those students having such peculiar interests. Such a suggestion has questionable presuppositions—even of a philosophical nature!—of which a person may not be aware. Usually when such a suggestion is made (perhaps in a curriculum committee meeting?) it is offered as a blanket statement and not as the conclusion of an argument, i.e., not in terms of evidence. In short, the question is begged. If we turn to the evidence, the matter is somewhat different. It is certainly true that the student should not be required to study systematically everything that may be relevant to, and may with profit be brought into, his various courses. There simply is not enough time, hence any curriculum must always leave out that which, all other things being equal, may be desirable to know. For example, a history teacher may find it most helpful to introduce, where relevant, some meteorology into his course, and about which subject he knows something. But from this fact alone, to insist that all students must study meteorology would hardly be justified. Does not the same hold true in connection with philosophy? No, and for at least three reasons.

In the first place, the argument plays upon the notion of knowledge in the abstract and fails to take into account the role a given kind of knowledge plays in a liberal education. As we have seen, philosophy has a unique and an essential function in liberal education, in eliminating shallowness and giving it depth. The fact that both philosophy and meteorology are introduced into a course is only an abstract similarity. What is important are the different reasons for "bringing them in." Philosophy, as we have seen, is *necessary* for a liberal education because through it two of the three meanings of "why" are introduced. This is not true in the case of meteorology. The introduction of meteorology into a course may be desirable, but not necessary in the same sense as philosophy.

Secondly, the human being is forced, of necessity, to make philosophical judgments in the activities of living, whereas such necessity may or may not be found in other kinds of knowledge. A person may be forced to make mathematical judgments, but not forced in the same way to make meteorological judgments. And he may never be forced in the least degree to make seismological judgments. But the matter is different in the case of philosophy, which includes such disciplines as logic, ethics, esthetics, epistemology (theory of knowledge), and metaphysics (or ontology, if that word is preferred).

One cannot live without thinking. The alternatives are only how relatively well or badly this is done. To require that a student study logic is simply to demand that he does relatively well that which he must do anyway. Again, one cannot live without making moral judgments. To demand that the student have some minimal knowledge of the ethical wisdom of mankind is simply to ask that the student perfect himself in that which of necessity he will do. In this way the student learns what he and his fellow men are doing in making moral appraisals—and an indefinite quantity of them are made daily. The student will also understand "why."

Such necessity for philosophical study does not differ from that for the study of mathematics or the study of nature in a scientific way. However, philosophy is peculiar in having a double necessity because of the nature of its subject matter. It is intrinsic to the very nature and definition of philosophy that it is concerned—together with theology—with that which is most important to man. Hence, *it is all the more necessary* for the student to study philosophy, to study rigorously and systematically that which deals with what is of most importance, in order to be free from, and not a slave to, the arbitrariness of subjectivism.

To mention the third reason for the inadequacy of this alternative will be perhaps anticlimactic by now. How can the student know philosophy by merely picking it up here and there in various nonphilosophical courses? It is granted that in the early years this is the way it *is* done. Furthermore, during the years of conscious *emphasis* on liberal education, that is the way it *may* be done in classrooms. But this cannot be sufficient if liberal education is taken seriously. Is the student never to study mathematics systematically, but only pick it up when it is "brought in" in science classes? But, then, why have science classes? Why not have students pick up their mathematics and science in, say, history classes —for doesn't history deal with the history of both mathematics and science. But, then, why study history? What is lacking in such reasoning is a foundation in the order of knowledge in which fundamental kinds of knowledge and their relationships to each other can be recognized. Also, the relative importance of kinds of knowledge is not recognized. Such importance, however, is not an arbitrary matter, not a matter of subjective appraisal. The importance of philosophy lies in the fact that it is concerned with that which is of most importance.

There is, then, no adequate alternative to courses in philosophy, i.e., to systematic studies, if the student is to obtain a liberal education. What happens more often than not, *in practice*, is that one may try to have both horns of the contradiction. Since this is theoretically impossible, it comes about and is sustained by an eclectic operation of the school. The faculty, or a faculty committee, simply votes in certain courses as nonelective, leaving out philosophy, and simply *says* that the result is a liberal education. In this expression of the "might makes right" doctrine there is the priority of power (votes) over norms. The norms are created by power instead of power being guided by norms. They are unaware that they are dealing with a problem of the philosophy of education, and that they are presupposing philosophy—however questionable it may be—in their act of voting. In fact, and perhaps of necessity, they are not prepared to give even a philosophical justification of the committee's actions. If all of this is pointed out to them, there are some who, because of bad faith, because of a pride that can see such an appeal as only that which makes them lose face, become positively embarrassed. Since the educator, being human, is not a purely intellectual creature, but has a will and emotions, this means that the correct understanding of education can never be a purely intellectual matter.

Finally, we come back to the problem of Mr. Smith and the other teachers who introduce philosophy into their courses. Should *they* have studied philosophy systematically in order to help the student obtain a liberal education? The answer, of course, must be in the affirmative, and no additional analysis is needed. A teacher can attempt to bring philosophy into a course without knowing too well what he is doing. In fact, in current education this is more often than not what is done. Not knowing logic—which word is *not* a synonym for mathematics—a teacher may, in bringing "it" into a course in mathematics tend to identify the two. Often in the teaching of English, a teacher may indulge in "philosophizing," the result being that the students are subjected to a mixture of half-truths, distorted truths, truths, prejudices, and personal ideology. The whole brew may be dished out with a certain linguistic persuasiveness, and which if sprinkled with the pepper of a few jokes is swallowed unknowingly but with pleasure by students, however questionable it may all be as intellectual food.

If the teacher is to help the student acquire a liberal education, to become at least intellectually free, then he himself must be free in the same sense. For he cannot responsibly teach what he does not know. Without a systematic study of philosophy there is an indefinite series of generation after generation of teachers, each one "picking up" some philosophy from the teacher before him. This is simply not taking philosophy seriously *as knowledge*; perhaps it should be called by some other name, that which we have mentioned before, a personal and/or collectivistic ideology.

A summary statement can now be made to the questions as to who is to teach philosophy and how it is to be done. A qualified philosopher should teach philosophy, in addition to the other teachers introducing the subject into their special subject matter courses. And it is to be taught systematically through courses in the various philosophical disciplines.

A person who has been somewhat "cut" by this analysis, and yet has a sense of humor sufficient to transcend the pain, might point out that perhaps philosophers themselves must share the blame if educational practice does not recognize that which *must* be recognized. The point is well taken.

Not only is this true, but it is also an excellent example of an understatement.

3

THE MATERIAL CAUSE: SOME MORAL RELATIONS BETWEEN TEACHER AND STUDENT

Among the various kinds of causes in the teacher-student relationship, the "material cause"—to use classical and technical language—is the student. But he is not just an object or thing to be molded, *that which* one acts upon. Because he is a person he is *who* the teacher acts upon. The sculptor respects the nature of the marble only for his, the sculptor's, purpose. The teacher, on the other hand, respects the nature and being of the student because of the student's purpose, namely, that of learning.

In the order of teaching and learning the interpretation of the material cause in terms of an analogy with the artist and his material is inadequate, because incomplete, and for three reasons. (1) The artist, say, a sculptor, deals with a "what." And so does a teacher, the "what" in this case being human nature. But the teacher also—and this is most important—deals with a "who," for the student is a person. (2) As an efficient cause, the teacher can be said to cause learning in the student. But it is also true that the student is himself an efficient cause in his own learning. (3) Since the teaching-learning activity is an interaction between persons, and hence between two efficient causes, there is a moral and ethical problem in such activity. Between a sculptor and his "material" there are no respective rights and duties. It is necessary to understand the mutual rights and duties of teacher and student. This chapter is concerned essentially with this matter.

The teaching activity has been expressed as follows: T teaches K_1 to S, by (means of) M, and for (the end) E. A teacher teaches a certain kind of knowledge to a student, by a certain means, and for a certain end. From the standpoint of learning we can say that a student learns a certain kind of knowledge from his teacher, by a certain means, and for a certain end. This may be formalized as follows: S learns K_1 from T by (means of) M, and (the end) E. We have seen that teaching is a triadic relation. Is learning triadic also? Appearances might lead one to assume so, but an analysis will show otherwise. Learning is a diadic relation.

One cannot teach without having a live student, but a student can learn without a live teacher. First, he can learn from a remote teacher, the author of a book, one who may not be living. Second, the student can learn, i.e., have certain basic forms of experience, without either a present or a remote teacher; for example, he may learn that fire can cause pain if he puts his hand in it. Although it is not recommended that he learn in this manner, he can do so. However, in other than primitive forms of learning he will need a teacher, and from the standpoint of schooling—and that is what our problem is about—he will need a live and present teacher, for a remote one is not sufficient.

Whereas, relative to teaching, the student is a "material" cause, in relation to learning the teacher is an efficient cause. The live, present teacher is one means, among others, by which the student gets to know a certain kind of knowledge. Hence, a verbal or symbolic reformulation is necessary in order to eliminate false appearances: S learns K_1, by (means of) M, and for (the end) E. Where now is "T"? The teacher is part of the means M. There can be many means by which a student learns—books, tape recordings, movies, teachers, etc. Here a distinction must be made between a necessary and a contingent means. In schooling, i.e., in institutionalized learning, a teacher is necessary. Such necessity does not apply to, say, movies. They may or may not be used, and hence are a contingent means. In fact, it is the teacher, a necessary means, who uses the other means which are contingent to help the student learn.

In the teacher-student relation, in the activity of teaching and learning, the locus of the material cause must be the student. Is, then, the student to the teacher as marble is to the sculptor? Yes and no. Yes, in the sense that both the student and the marble represent the same kind of cause, in distinction from other kinds, but not in the same way.

There are certain similarities. Both the sculptor and the teacher must know the nature of the "raw material" they are working with. The sculptor can do certain things with marble that he cannot do with clay; and conversely. What kind of marble is it? He must know its grain and how to prevent undue chipping, etc. Likewise, the teacher must know the student, *who* he is, if he is to help him learn. Of course, in mass education there can only be a rough approximation to such knowledge. Yet such knowledge is a necessity for the perfection of teaching. If the student is to be helped to get to know some kind of knowledge, then the teacher should know what, at any time, the student already knows and does not know. Otherwise the student will see no link, no connection between what he already knows and that which he is encouraged to get to know. Parenthetically, it may be remarked that this was one of the main points in the pedagogical theory of John Dewey and some of his followers. The denial of this reduces learning, sense II, to learning, sense I, and the latter is learning in the sense of parroting. Also, the teaching of the teacher is reduced to simply "telling" the student, and hence pedagogy, sense II, is reduced to pedagogy, sense I. The two senses of pedagogy (teaching) are correlative with the two senses of learning mentioned by Mr. Castell.

Not only should the teacher know what the student does and does not in fact know, but he should also know the potentialities of the student. This requires that the teacher not only know human nature in general, but also, to the degree possible, the individual nature of each student. The capacity, the ability of a student makes learning possible and at the same time limits its extent. As is well known, it is very difficult for a teacher to acquire such knowledge, and at best it is only some kind of statistical approximation. But to the extent that the individual student's capabilities can be discerned, two errors can be avoided—underestimating or overestimating a student's capacity to learn. In the one case a teacher may hold a student back on his learning activities; and in the other case, push too hard and too fast.

In a sense there is a violation of the person to the degree that the teacher does not know the mind of the student. For the student tends to become something like the marble in the hands of the sculptor. To the degree that the teacher merely "tells" the student, and the student merely parrots, then the student really never "gets to know," although he may "get to behave" in a certain way, and have caused in him certain attitudes. In fact, this almost defines propaganda in the negative sense of the term. A certain kind of advertising may tell a person what to do, what attitudes to have, and through such conditioning a person may perform in that manner without having the slightest idea why he acts the way he does, or whether he should act that way.

A totalitarian regime extends and perfects such conditioning. As we have seen earlier, conditioning and teaching are quite different from each other. To identify them would be to reduce the teaching relation from a triadic to a diadic relation, for conditioning is the latter.

Although the sharpness of these distinctions can be made theoretically, in practice good and bad teaching is a matter of degree, and is also sometimes related to the kind of subject matter being taught. In a strictly totalitarian regime there may be relatively good teaching in a technical subject, say, engineering. Here we may find pedagogy, sense II. Yet in political science or philosophy, if they can be said to exist at all, there is pedagogy, sense I. But this, which might characterize the "education" in such a regime, may be found in various places in democratic countries, relatively localized and as yet unorganized.

Although both the sculptor and the teacher have in common the necessity of knowing their material cause, i.e., the raw material with which they are to work, since the material cause for the teacher is a *person* the necessity becomes also an ethical obligation and not merely an esthetic demand, as it is for the sculptor.

Although there is an art in teaching, the differences between artist and teacher are more important than the similarities. In the first place, as has been shown, both student and marble are *that which* is acted upon. But the student is not a mere *that which*, not merely a physical object. Being a person the student is also a "who." Second, the marble remains passive under the tools of the sculptor in the creation of the statue. The student is active. He must desire to learn, and actively do so, for no one else can learn for him. He can only be helped. Part of the art of teaching lies in discovering the various ways of motivating a student.

Thirdly, the most important difference between artist and teacher, we have mentioned before, is that, whereas the sculptor has an esthetic interest in the shaping of the marble, the teacher has an ethical obligation in helping him to learn. There is a great deal of difference between saying that there is an art to teaching and saying that the teacher is an artist. He cannot be an artist, for in the very attempt to become an artist he would cease to be a teacher. The student is a person *who* has a nature which is to be perfected in the way of knowing. The student is not just "stuff" to be molded or shaped into an artifact according to the purposes of the teacher.

If all this is denied, then a kind of knowledge is reduced to ideology; the teacher becomes a technician propagandizing for personal and/or social ideological purposes; the student becomes an object, a thing; learning becomes parroting (the teacher's or the Party's "line"); and the teaching activity is reduced from the triadic to the diadic relation, that of conditioning or determining the student in a subintellectual manner.

It is important to note that such reductionism, which may be correctly called a kind of teaching-learning nihilism, does not at all require that all parroting be that of falsehoods and nonsense statements. There can be a parroting of truths, there can be the conditioning of a student in the accepting of truths. A great deal of this may have to be done in the early years, but the whole aim of a correct kind of education is to get the child past this stage. Otherwise, he remains a child. To give a rather extreme example merely to get the point across, perhaps there is little more a teacher or a parent can do than to tell (require) a two-year-old child not to run into the street. To explain "why" in terms of getting hurt may not mean very much; nor would a further "why" in terms of physics, the relation to each other of mass bodies—the automobile and the child—be relevant. At this stage of a child's life, "telling," together with the threat of possible punishment—all of which is a kind of conditioning in a nonintellectual manner—may be justified by the fact that the aim is to have the child live long enough so that later he can understand and know the "why." For the same reason, we require the child to eat certain kinds of foods, or take certain kinds of medicine.

The reductionism of which we have spoken—especially that of reducing the student to an object, a thing—may be illustrated by reference to the Nazi regime in Germany. We do this somewhat apologetically, not because there is any question as to the intrinsic evil of the regime, but rather because of the danger of self-righteousness. (It is always psychologically efficacious to choose an example of badness far back in time and distance from one's own shores. A current example at home might produce psychological obstacles to understanding.) We choose the Nazi regime as an example chiefly because it is a safe one. If a less clear-cut one were used, then psychologically—even though there is no logical connection whatsoever—the inadequacy or questionableness of the example would likely be taken as evidence against the principle illustrated.

In Nazi "education," there was not only the "teaching" of falsehoods and nonsense sentences (for these could not be propositions or statements), but also the teaching of truths. No person and no state utters only nontruths. To believe otherwise is to underestimate the cleverness of evil wills. The greatest error is a deliberate half-truth or the distortion of a whole truth. It is also the most dangerous, for its partial truth is just sufficient to persuade the intellectually unsophisticated. That Jesus was not a Jew is false; that the Nordic race is superior is not false, but nonsense, for it is not even a proposition. The notion of a "Nordic race" is a contradiction in itself. A proposition must be meaningful in order that it can be potentially true or false. A child might be taught that "black tastes worse than red." Although this is nonsense, and is neither true nor false, it is conceivable that, after years of parroting this, the child may have acquired certain hostile attitudes towards, say, Negroes. But this would not be possible unless the nonsense were related to true propositions which the child truly learned, e.g., that there are black people.

And so, in Nazi nontechnical "education," nonsense was combined with many truths; e.g., that there is much corruption in capitalism and democracy, something few would be so bold as to deny. But the student was never allowed to understand why, he was merely told *that*. But even this is not sufficient to violate the person of the student and reduce him to a thing. What accomplished this was the shaping of the student through the creation of attitudes, so that not only was the student denied the possibility of understanding why, but was also penalized for the attempt.

What is relevant is the question of whether the corruption of democracy is intrinsic to it. If not, then the solution is to perfect democracy, not destroy it. That the Nazi student was in fact not allowed to think about such questions was not merely a matter of educational fault or mistake—for no educational system is perfect. No, it was rather that such "education" *could* not allow it. To be used as an instrument for Nazi purposes, it was intrinsic to the nature of Nazism that it could not allow the student to learn in certain respects, one of which was understanding the meaning of Nazism itself. It was this that reduced the student to a thing, a mere instrument. In order to train young people to violate the personality of others, it was first necessary to violate, through "education," the personalities of the students themselves.

The teacher-student relationship is thus not merely a logical one, mediated by the kind of knowledge the teacher teaches and the student is supposed to learn. It is at least that, but it is also a moral relationship. In fact, it *must* be a moral relationship, and both teaching and learning are ineffective to the extent that the moral is lacking. Let us turn to the evidence to see why this is so.

Justice is a virtue concerned with the action of one person upon another, and hence is relevant to the teacher-student relationship. It should, we say, be a just, not an unjust, one. This may mean many things. For the purpose of analyzing the moral nature of the relationship let us consider one problem and pursue it, namely, academic freedom. The student must be free to learn and the teacher must be free to teach. Each has the duty to respect the freedom and the rights of the other. To rescue such statements from the charge of being rather empty tautologies, it will be necessary to digress and consider the nature of rights and duties. After having done so, we shall apply the principle to the teacher-student relationship. Such a digression would not be necessary were it not for the fact that our contemporary moral terms such as "justice," "rights," and "freedom" have so often been reduced to ideological weapons that it has become increasingly difficult to communicate intelligibly about them. In fact, with the rapid decline of any systematic moral education in recent times, many people, even of actual or potential goodwill, are acquainted only with these moral terms in their corrupted meanings. What follows is not meant to be an exhaustive treatment, just the minimum is necessary to clarify the nature of academic freedom.

A "right," whatever more it may be, is at least a claim upon the actions of other people. In that sense, if I have a right, then of necessity it limits the absoluteness of the actions of others and renders them "relative." But if others have rights, then they make a claim upon me and my absoluteness. There are certain things I may and may not do. The recognition of mutual claims, of rights, introduces the notion of "duty." My right may be your duty. If I have the right to walk freely, innocent of violating any laws or of harming others, then it becomes your duty to allow me to do so. If my right is not respected by others, then in fact I do not have the right except in a theoretical sense. My right exists concretely in the world to the extent that others recognize it by limiting their actions with respect to me. Such limitations become their duties. It is in this sense that duties and rights are correlative. (In another sense they are not correlative. For example, a person may have the right to social-security payments, but he cannot be said to have a duty to accept them.)

Correlative terms are those that mutually require each other—husband and wife, captain and crew, east and west, rights and duties. If I were to say that everyone is a husband, it would make no sense, for if there are no wives there can be no husbands. If I were to say that everything is east, and there is no west, then I would be playing with words. East of what? Just east! Now, if I were to say that everyone has rights but no duties, then I would be saying, not something that is false, but rather uttering a sentence (and, grammatically, it could be a good English sentence) that from the standpoint of truth-meaning is nonsensical. For, if everyone had rights, and no one had duties, then there could be neither rights nor duties.

There are two kinds of rights, one being prior to, and the other being a product of, society or the state. The terms "society" and "state" are not to be equated, but we shall use either one, indifferently, if in context the difference is not relevant. In ethical theory and jurisprudence, the first kind is called a "natural right," and the second, a "positive right." These terms correspond to "natural law" and "positive law." An example of a natural right is one's right to life. An example of a positive right is one's right to receive social-security payments. A natural right is not created by the state and given to the individual. Rather, the individual person has it prior to, i.e., independent of, the state, and it is the moral duty of the state to recognize it. A positive right, on the other hand, is given and recognized by the state precisely because the state has created it. The state does not, and cannot, create one's life, one's being; hence has no right to take the life of an innocent person. A natural right one has at all times and at all places, and since it is not man-made it cannot be man-changed. Furthermore, it applies to everyone, regardless of worldly status. Whether the White House janitor murders the President of the United States, or the President murders the janitor, the act is equally wrong whichever the case may be. If the President were the guilty one and, because of his power and position, escaped all legal procedures, then we would say that an injustice has been done.

Positive law and positive rights are man-made and can be man-changed. They may vary from time to time and from place to place. At one time people of a certain age in the United States did not have social-security rights. These were created later and people now have these rights. Prior to 1919, women in the United States did not have the right to vote; but now they do. In Switzerland, women neither then nor now have the right to vote. But a person's natural right to life is not a function of the state, or of socialization. A woman had the right to life before 1919 and has it now. If innocent, harming no one nor violating any law, she has this right to life whether she is walking in Central Park in New York, down the street in London, or through the forests of Brazil. To kill her would be morally wrong regardless of the motive whether it be robbery, rape, or some other. This truth is independent of geography, but it is the duty of the various societies in different places to recognize it. This may be done by creating a positive right founded upon the natural right. In this case, it then becomes illegal to commit murder. Murder is wrong. But the order of causality must be respected. Murder is illegal because it is morally wrong; it is not morally wrong because it is illegal. The inversion of this order makes possible a person such as Eichmann, the Nazi gauleiter, for whom murder, the killing of innocent Jews, was not illegal at all.

All rights, natural or positive, are limited according to the duties correlative to them. This can be misunderstood. The limitation is completely nonarbitrary. It is something "built in," so to speak, intrinsic to the very nature of a right, and which prevents it from being a "fiction" or a "fictitious right." In future years, I may have the right to draw social-security payments. I now have a number. But this right is contingent, hence limited, by my duty to make contributions to the system. If I do not do my duty, then I forfeit my right. I cannot have it both ways. This is not at all changed by the fact that a person, by some special law, might be allowed to receive such payments. If so, it would be an example of a privilege, not a right. To insist upon a right without taking account of the responsibilities and duties that make the right possible, is simply to make noise or emotionally express a wish. In fact, one turns the right into a fiction, for it can't be a reality. It is in this sense, but only in this sense, that there are no absolute rights, i.e., rights without duties.

There are those who deny that there are any natural rights. There is nothing new about this, since almost anything and everything has been asserted or denied at one time or another. However, it is not always clear exactly what it is that is denied. The doctrine of natural law has a long and ancient heritage, and it has been expressed and justified in many ways. Sometimes natural law has been unconsciously identified with some particular expression of it, e.g., that of Locke or Hobbes, and the inadequacy of their positions is taken as evidence against the very concept of natural rights. But evidence against a position which explains the "why," the ontological foundation of natural rights, is not necessarily evidence against the fact *that* they are. Rather, any ontological position on natural rights presupposes them in the same sense that one cannot have a theory about fossils without presupposing their existence.

If there are literally no natural rights in any sense at all, then there is only the positive law. Since this is now absolute, it becomes an "ism," and hence has been called "legal positiv*ism*." But legal positivism is not so much an explanation of, as it is the denial of, the virtue of justice, for then there are no norms based upon the nature of man and the "nature of things" which are transcendent to, and can be the judge of, the positive law of given societies. The legal positivist may insist that he, too, is talking about justice, but that it is merely a different theory. But this cannot be the case if his position requires the denial of the very reality that the natural law doctrine is about. It would be more accurate to say, we suggest, that the legal positivist, while denying the *concept* of justice as one of the cardinal virtues, still insists on using the *word*, "justice."

There are those, however, who know exactly what they are doing when they deny even the possibility of natural rights. If a naturalistic or materialistic ontology be given as a posit, then it can be deduced that there can be no natural rights. Nature is "all there is," and man is taken to be no more than a bio-social creature. There are other ways of deducing that there can be no natural rights. But at least the naturalist or materialist is formally consistent, and in that respect he is clear. He does not confuse the issue by trying to have it both ways, which is so often the case with that kind of skeptic or agnostic who is so "liberal" that he lacks the courage of consistency. In the case of the materialist, there is no problem of whether or not natural rights exist, hence one cannot discuss it with him. For the issue has shifted and, if there is to be any discussion at all, it can only be on that which is relevant, namely, the question of the truth or falsity of materialism itself.

We are assuming, though not arbitrarily, that there are natural rights. We assume, to put it crudely, that it makes sense to say that murder is illegal *because* it is morally wrong; and that, other than as a morbid witticism, it does not make *cognitive* sense to assert the converse. At present we are assuming only *that* there are natural rights, and not an ontological position explaining them. It will be recognized that this assumption is not arbitrary relative to our problem. Without this assumption, there simply would be no problem of just relations between teacher and student. One would have to say that "justice" is whatever is in accordance with the positive law in different societies. All that is left is a statistical sociological study of what *in fact* exists in teacher-student relationships in various places.

Let us now return to the problem of academic freedom. Is it necessary, or merely desirable? Does it exist for the teacher only? Or for the student too? And what duties go with this kind of freedom?

Let us begin by considering academic freedom as it applies to the student. So often this notion is thought of only in connection with teaching. But there is a freedom to learn as well as to teach. In fact, as we shall see, they mutually imply each other. After all, the school exists primarily for the student, not the teacher.

The student cannot effectively learn without the freedom to learn, and that freedom is not something to be tolerated in a negative manner, but rather something to be actively encouraged and developed. Is this a natural right or merely a positive right? It is primarily a natural right, and, because it is so, it is concretized through law and becomes also a positive right. If freedom to learn is not a natural right, then no matter how much a given society may restrict children in learning, it could not be criticized, for if positive law is absolute there is nothing transcending it in terms of which it could be criticized. One would have to remain silent or indifferent and retreat to one's preferences. Society X does not allow the freedom to learn. I live in society Y which has the freedom. The most I could say would be that I *prefer* a society that has the freedom. But if so, then I am restricted to talking about myself, i.e., my own preferences, which is something quite different from making a moral judgment.

The freedom to learn remains an abstraction, however, unless it is further qualified. It is the limitation of a right that makes it both possible and concrete, and without which it becomes a fiction, its use a slogan. The student has a right to learn what? The answer to this depends upon what is meant by the question. In the abstract, the answer perhaps is that the student has the right to learn anything that is or can be known. Concretely and in practice, however, i.e. what is existentially relevant to schooling, the answer must be more specific. The student should be free to learn whatever he can, depending on his age and knowledge-level. It is not very clear what meaning it would have to say that a student in the first grade has the freedom to learn differential equations when he does not even know his numbers as yet. Is such a child to be free also to learn the function of sex in marriage? The examples are extreme but they serve to point up the principle involved. The student cannot be said to have a right to learn about such matters *at that age and that knowledge-level*. But it can be said that the student has that right in the sense that he should be able to pursue his education up the education ladder so that at some place along the way he *can* learn about such matters with some degree of profit. Just *when* it is best to try to learn about such matters may be difficult to determine, hence is somewhat of a variable. But this would not even be a problem were it not that the principle is true and is a constant.

The student has duties as well as rights, for the two cannot be separated. If he has the right to learn, then he has the duty to continue to merit the right. But how is this possible, it may be asked. If the child has the freedom to learn, as a right prior to the learning activity precisely because he is a human being, then how can such a right be contingent upon such an activity? Is there not a contradiction here? It would seem to be so unless there is a proper understanding. Since this has sometimes been lacking, the consequences can and have been an educational romanticism. Clarification is necessary.

A person *has* a natural right because of his *being*, because of *what* and *who* he is, and not because of what he *does*. But whether or not he *continues* to have it does depend on what he does. *Being* and *doing* are not the same and are distinct, but it does not follow that in the activities of living they have no relation at all. Were it not so, a natural right not only would be irrelevant to human conduct, but also would be unrelated to duties. Prior to what a person does, and because of his being, he has the natural right to life. My natural right to life implies your duty to respect it. But I, too, have a duty that goes with my right to life, namely, to respect your right to life in my *doing*, my conduct. If I kill an innocent person, then I forfeit my right. *I continue to merit my right to life, which right I had prior to my conduct, only so long as my conduct reflects the duty implied by the right, namely, that I respect the rights of others and do not commit murder.* Society or the state may or may not take the life I have forfeited. If it does, it is called "capital punishment." It does not follow that, if I forfeit my right to life, the state must necessarily take my life. Maybe it shouldn't. Perhaps there are better ways of dealing with the matter. This raises the issue of capital punishment as a moral *means*. But there would be nothing to debate on the level of means if the principle were not admitted that I forfeit my right to life unless I continue to merit it by doing my duty and respecting the equal natural rights of others.

The freedom to learn is a natural right. In fact, it is a species of the more general category "the right to life." This is sometimes forgotten, because in discussing one mode of negating the right, namely, murder, one may unconsciously limit the meaning of the right to mere biological survival. However, the right means a great deal more than this, for it is a human right and a human activity that must be understood on its own level. Now, one kind of human activity, one which is uniquely human, is the acquisition of knowledge. Without doing so, one cannot perfect one's own nature, cannot live on a human level. Hence, the freedom to learn is a natural right, part of what is included within the more general natural right, the right to life. For part of *human* living is human learning. And so the student has as a natural right the freedom to learn.

However, the student also has a duty that goes with the right. In this case, he has the duty to exercise continuously the right that he has. Otherwise, he forfeits his right. An analogous example on the physiological level would not be that of murder, which is the example we have used, but rather that of not eating correctly. One has the right to life, but he also has the duty continuously to merit that right by eating the proper foods. If he does not do so, then he may forfeit his life—which means that he dies, for Nature respects man's freedom, even the abuse of it, and allows the consequences of his actions logically to take their course.

And so the student has the duty continuously to exercise his right to learn. Otherwise, he foreits his right. But a right to what? At this point it would be dangerous to get into the rut of analogous reasoning in which similarities are stressed to the point of overlooking differences. The truth about every kind of natural right must rest on evidence intrinsic to its own nature. Now there is a difference. Does not the student have the right to learn, the freedom to learn, regardless of whether or not at any given time he exercises his right, whether or not he does his duty? Yes and no, depending upon what exactly is meant.

The answer must be affirmative in one sense. In the case of murder or the wrong eating of foods, one's natural right to life is forfeited because one's *being* is totally negated, which being is the foundation of the natural right to life. However, if a student does not do his duty and exercise his right to learn, he does not totally negate his being, however much he may corrupt it. He lives on in his being, and so long as he lives he has all the natural rights that his being confers upon him, including the freedom to learn. In this sense, the student retains his natural right to learn even though he does not do his duty. He has not totally negated his being. He has rather negated the perfection of his being, hence may be said to be foolish. This is the penalty attached to the separation of rights and duties on the part of the student. For, if morally they cannot be separated, then of necessity some evil must eventuate if they are.

But there is another penalty attached. If the student does not wholly lose his natural right to learning because his total being has not been negated, nevertheless he may forfeit his *positive* right, which society has given him, to remain in school. What the school can do is to give the student an educational opportunity, and to do what it can to encourage the student to make use of it. Even an education-failure still retains his natural right to learn; but he cannot continuously demand that the school give him the opportunity to learn unless, to some degree, he performs his duties and makes use of such an opportunity. And this has at least two implications: (1) any given student may not have the right to move up the educational ladder, but rather may quite legitimately be shunted off into some elementary vocational education; (2) it may be the case that a student, and again quite legitimately, ought to be a "drop-out." Neither the student nor his parents has a right to demand continuous schooling unless the student performs the duty which is correlative to his right. Not to recognize this is to spoil and miseducate the student. At best, this is educational romanticism, not realism; at worst, it implicitly, if not explicitly, reduces the student's personality to an instrument.

With regard to students' rights and duties, further qualifications are necessary because we have not as yet taken into account the question of age. Students may be of almost any age. There are no students "in general." Can these principles to which we refer apply equally, and in the same way, to a first grader, a student in the 15th grade, and to a graduate student in a university? They apply, yes, but not equally and in the same way.

A student has a natural right to learn regardless of whether he is aware of it or not. He has the right in virtue of his being, not his subjectivity. This is true for anyone at whatever age; it can be true for a positive right also.

A person may have the right to social-security payments, and yet not be aware of it. This sometimes happens. In the case of natural rights, the same may be the case. Perhaps only a few sophisticates are self-consciously aware of the fact that they have them. Other people are more or less conscious that they have them, though they may not be familiar with the language in terms of which they are discussed, in the same sense in which they know that they breathe, and that it is good, without knowing much more about it. Finally, there are those who, because of age and development, lack any awareness at all, e.g., a baby.

All human beings have natural rights, independent of awareness. A person cannot kill a baby and then plead no murder by pointing out that the baby was unaware of its right to life. A person must respect the baby's natural right to life. The protection of such a right becomes the parent's duty, and when the baby grows up he becomes aware of the right that was so protected. But up to a certain age, and that may be a variable, a child can be said to have a natural right and at the same time no obligation to perform the duties which go with that right. But, once again, since rights and duties cannot be wholly separated—for otherwise each would be reduced to fiction—wherein lies the locus of duty? It has to be somewhere. It lies with the parents. It is for this reason that, if a 5-year-old child grabs a gun, shoots, and kills another person, neither the death penalty nor any other is inflicted upon him. Instead, the parents are blamed for allowing him to acquire the weapon. Just where the age of innocence ends and that of responsibility begins is difficult to say with accuracy, and a social order usually has to be satisfied with a good statistical guess. But the validity of the distinction remains.

And so it is with schooling. A child does not know that he has a natural right to learn, nor is he aware of the correlative duties. It is the duty of the parents, through the social institution of the school, to see that the child exercises his right in so far as he is able. In so doing, a duty is placed upon the teacher also to help in his professional capacity. He must exercise this duty in at least two ways.

In the first place, especially with students below what is called the age of responsibility, the teacher has a duty to exercise those arts of persuasion and techniques of motivation which will help cause a student to desire and to enjoy learning, thus enabling the student to make the most of the opportunity which is his right. Second, although these pedagogical arts are to be used at all levels of education, as the students move up the educational ladder there is an additional duty on the part of the teacher and the school. Practically, the student should be introduced to a *knowledge* of his rights and duties with respect to education, not only to the knowledge *that* he has them but also *why* he has them. When this is fully and consciously done, it will constitute part of that liberal education which is necessary to the perfection of a person. Also a change will take place in the locus of duties. What at one time was solely the duty of parents and teachers now gradually shifts to the student. Even though the duties of the teacher continue, the student now takes upon himself, gradually to be sure, the duty of exercising his freedom to learn. If he does not do so, then the blame and the guilt fall increasingly upon him and there comes a time when justice may demand that he be denied, not his natural right to learn, but his positive right to educational opportunity to learn in school. Equality of educational opportunity, as a natural right, does not by itself alone guarantee forever equality in schooling, independent of what the student does and regardless of merit. The truth of this is independent of the fact that, in any given case, the judgment of the authorities is always a matter of prudential decision, and may be difficult to make.

The activities of learning and teaching are so closely related that in considering the rights and duties of the student we have already had to mention the duties of the teacher. What does it mean for a teacher to have academic freedom? In what sense is it a right? And what duties go with it?

The student's duty to learn implies the teacher's freedom to teach the kind of knowledge the student is supposed to learn. The obviousness of this in principle is likely to blunt awareness of the fact that this is not always observed in practice, especially in the teaching of "controversial subjects." The right to teach also implies the right to have others respect his authority in his own field of knowledge in so far as he knows it. In any given case, of course, this may be difficult to determine. It means at least this, however, that the teacher should be free of social pressures which would require him to distort or withhold relevant knowledge in a course. For example, in a class in "agriculture" in college, the truth about margarine and butter should not be withheld because a member of the board of trustees owns a dairy business and has indirectly been concerned about "what has been going on in a certain class." Even in more controversial subjects, usually those called "value subjects," the teacher must have freedom to teach within the restrictions set by the kind of knowledge he is supposed to teach. To rescue this from an innocuous truism, it is necessary to point out that this freedom makes quite a demand upon the teacher, for to know the limitations of his own special subject is to have a kind of knowledge other than that subject. The judgment of how well this principle is acted upon, whether made by the teacher or by his superior, will turn out to be prudential, and often a matter of debate.

Does a teacher have the right to teach any truth even in his own subject matter? A simple illustration will point up the prudential aspect. Let us suppose a teacher of the second grade, in the course of dealing with the history of the Colonies and with George Washington, stresses the fact that Washington wrote love letters to another man's wife, and made some money in shady land deals. When the protests come in from parents, he pleads academic freedom. Is it justified? The issue is not the truth of the statements, but rather whether he should tell *those* truths. Are no truths to be withheld from a student at any age? If one maintained this, then he would have to hold that the age-level of the student is irrelevant to what may be taught—which, of course, is admittedly a false proposition. It would seem, then, that prudence demands the withholding of truths at certain ages, the reason being the danger that their presentation at a given age may lead more to misunderstanding than to understanding. Is there any school, at any place in the world, and at any time, that has not done this?

This problem is a little more subtle than it appears. For one may ask whether it is justifiable to teach falsehoods, if they lead to more knowledge than not teaching them. The whole truth about Washington is not being presented, hence to that degree a relatively false image of Washington is being created in the minds of the students. Let us ask another question: can it be otherwise? What solution does the teacher really propose? Taken literally, it is a pure contradiction, hence nonsense, to say that a teacher's function is to teach falsehoods instead of truths. But is the selection of truths, that of not giving the whole truth, that kind of falsehood? In high school chemistry, the whole truth about valence cannot be told. The student really only understands it when he comes much later, if at all, to physical chemistry. Again, to make the problem more complicated, can something that is relatively false be used to communicate a truth? Obviously not. Yet, in the 1st or 2nd grade, look at the drawing of the earth going around the sun. It is a long ellipse with the foci far apart. Now the earth does not really move that way. If the drawing were accurate, the ellipse would be so close to a circle that in appearance the student would confuse it with a circle, hence not understand the elliptical orbit.

When it comes to matters of prudence, there are no rules for the automatic and simple solution of problems. Prudence is the virtue concerned with the art of applying principles. When singular cases of alleged infringement of academic freedom arise and call for judgment, then, however clear the right to teaching-freedom may be in principle, for better or worse that judgment must be prudential. Whatever uncertainty is involved usually stems from the complexity of the existential circumstances. And it cannot be mentioned too often, that in the absence of a great deal of moral integrity on the part of the teacher there can be no solutions to such problems.

Infringements upon the freedom of teaching are roughly proportional to the scale in the education ladder, being more frequent on the upper levels. There is a reason for this. As the student grows older and matures, he merits the right to learn that which, for prudential reasons, was withheld from him in the earlier years. As these truths gradually emerge in the teaching activity, there may arise pressures, social and otherwise, to have them suppressed. If so, then there is genuine interference with the freedom of teaching, which is not morally justifiable. But, even this cannot properly be understood unless the duties as well as the rights of the teacher are considered.

Pedagogical books are sometimes filled with detailed lists of what a teacher ought to do, including keeping a classroom well ventilated. Such a list of rules and duties has its function, and is not to be deprecated. But the problem here is concerned with the duties of a teacher in a more basic sense, having to do with ethical principles.

The first duty of a teacher is to "know his stuff." The school exists primarily for the student and not the teacher. The purpose of teaching is primarily to help the student to "get to know," to learn some specific kind of knowledge. The teacher was once a student, too, and had the freedom to learn. If he merits the right to teach, then he has of necessity acquired the knowledge which he hopes to convey to the student. The right to teach implies the duty to know one's special subject that is to be taught. If this seems like belaboring the obvious, it is sometimes forgotten that one may believe, sincerely but mistakenly, that he knows more than he really does. An example may illustrate. A very wealthy man, retired at an early age, was not only disappointed but somewhat offended because a business school would not give him the right to teach "marketing." Had he not made his fortune marketing the farm machinery of a certain manufacturer? Did he not know "marketing"? Of course, yes and no. What he failed to understand was that the subject included a lot more knowledge than he had.

The teacher has the duty, and not merely the right, to insist that what he teaches is knowledge, *in some sense or other*. And he should understand and be sensitive to the qualification. For there are "degrees of knowledge," and there are degrees of certainty based upon the extent of the evidence. He has the duty to separate good guesses and personal prejudice from opinions based on a modicum of evidence, and these in turn from propositions having a high probability of truth or having practical if not theoretical certainty. A proper understanding of this obligation would require him to have not merely a knowledge of his own special field, but also of that part of philosophy which is concerned with logic, epistemology, and the order of knowledge. At least, he should not be naive about these matters.

The teacher also has an obligation not only to know those

pedagogical methods that can help make him an effective teacher, but also to be alert to new techniques. This may not be necessary for a person in his role as a research worker, but it is his duty in so far as he is a teacher.

Also, a teacher has the obligation to recognize the authority of others in their own fields. This is a moral demand, and it requires some humility and self discipline on his part. An example may relieve the abstractness of this principle. In higher education, a professor of biology should not argue that to have peace there must be, of necessity, a world government; for nations are like cells in an organism, and if cells were separated from the organic whole there would be only disintegration and death, etc. etc. The reader may say that such "things" and their equivalents go on in classrooms all the time. Unfortunately, this is correct; which simply says that a great deal of immorality and intellectual nonsense goes on under the guise of teaching a kind of knowledge.

The exact issue here should be understood. The issue is not whether world government is desirable and is necessary to achieve peace in the world; nor is there any question about the right of the professor to know what he is talking about, and to know the limitations of his own special field. But there is a lack of justice in the classroom in such a leap from biology to international politics.

In the first place, he does not know where his subject begins and where it ends; for in advocating and trying to "prove" the necessity of world government he has stepped outside the field of biology, in which he is an authority, without warning the students of the fact. Thus, there is an illegitimate shift of authority. Second, he has used bad logic by using what is called a "false analogy," thus demonstrating his lack of knowledge of another field which he ought to know. Third, he has misled students into thinking that biology can prove more than it can, namely, that biological evidence can prove something in political science or international affairs—which, of course, is not merely false but plain nonsense. What the teacher is doing, then, is imposing his own ignorance on students under the guise of wisdom, and by virtue of his status he renders them rather helpless.

Helpless? Cannot the students protest, or at least correct him?

However innocent or naive the question is, the answer is yes. Since this is not a hypothetical example, one very brilliant student did attempt to correct him, and he "learned" the following—that there are two approaches, the biological and that of political science, that there is a difference of opinion on such matters, but that this is good, for it is the mark of a *live* university and surely the student would not want it otherwise.

Now, of course, that was the final sophistry. If that is multiplied by a few million, day in and day out, one may get a rather accurate image of contemporary education. These ethical principles we have stated, which are intrinsic to the very nature of teaching, may seem in the abstract to be truisms. Therefore, why belabor the obvious? They are truisms. However, when once the full implications are examined, it turns out that to many, if not to most, they are not at all immediately obvious; and perhaps they need some belaboring.

To be most effective as a teacher, one should have goodwill, be a seeker of truth, have intellectual humility. He should love his students as fellow human beings, and not use them as instruments of his egotism. And so on. If teaching is one kind of moral activity among others, then the teacher must be just, must be moral. It is not sufficient merely to have piled up credits in courses on "teaching."

Let us now turn to the most important difference between the teacher and the student with respect to academic freedom.

A student because he is a person has the natural right to learn, hence he must have the freedom to do so. If the student fails to exercise his freedom, he may lose his educational opportunity to schooling, but not totally his right to learn. A natural right is not man-made, and therefore cannot be destroyed. His right to schooling, however, is a man-made, positive right, and what is man-created and given to a person can also be taken away. On the other hand, the teacher, because he is a person, *does not have a natural right to teach*. Rather, his right to teach is a positive right which he has obtained through merit. The right of the student to learn is independent of merit, but not his right to stay in school. But in the case of the teacher both his right to teach and his opportunity to teach rests on merit, on whether he fulfills his duty. To the degree that this is not recognized in practice, there is injustice.

Expressing it another way, for the student, learning is a prior right he has because he is a person, and in exercising his right in schooling he does his duty. The teacher, on the other hand, merits his right to teach only in so far as he performs his duties. It is for this reason that the persistent concern of the teaching profession with the rights of teachers, without being equally clear and concerned about their duties, is evidence either of naivete, of ignorance, or of just plain bad faith.

4

KNOWLEDGE AS THE FORMAL CAUSE IN TEACHING AND LEARNING

In the teaching-learning causal complex it is knowledge that is the formal cause. In helping the student "get to know," the teacher intends to cause knowledge in the student; and to the extent that the effect occurs, the student learns. What is taught and what is learned may be totally dissimilar. The teacher may teach more than the student learns, and the student may learn more than the teacher teaches; but, if there is no similarity with respect to knowledge, then there would be no causal connection between teaching and learning. From the standpoint of the teacher, the student is the material cause. From the standpoint of the student, the teacher is an efficient cause. But knowledge is the *formal* cause from both standpoints.

As has been remarked before, we refer to knowledge in the broadest sense possible in relation to teaching. The qualification, "in relation to teaching," is important, for it defines the limitation of our problem although it does not define the limits of learning. One cannot teach what cannot be learned. But one can learn what cannot be taught. For example, a teacher can teach me something about children in general, and it is possible that he might even teach me something about my own child—if he were a psychologist. But there is that about my child which I know, and which no teacher could teach me. Were this not so, I could not learn about my child from a teacher. Another example: if God exists and has given some special revelation to some people, then they may teach others. But the knowledge they teach was not taught (humanly) to them.

It is understandable then that, in considering the nature of knowledge in the teacher-student relationship, our concern is necessarily limited to those kinds of knowledge that can be taught to the student and also can be learned by the student from the teacher. Even so, this should not be conceived too narrowly. It is sometimes said that there cannot be a science of any singular. Properly interpreted, this is correct. There can be no science of this blade of grass, this dog, this electron, or this person. Here "science" refers to the general universal (which can be taught), but it cannot exhaust the being of any singular existent. However, knowledge that can be taught is not limited to the general or universal in this sense. In fact, the primary function of the historian is to acquire knowledge about the uniqueness of events. A reconstruction of the life of George Washington is knowledge about *this* unique man, and not about men in general. And such knowledge can be taught. What should be realized is that Washington as a singular existent is neither limited to, nor exhausted by, such knowledge.

It may be well to digress a bit here and admit again to certain assumptions that will be found in this chapter and, in part, are presupposed throughout this study of the order of teaching and learning. Any limited study always makes assumptions; it could not be otherwise. What is relevant and important is: Are such assumptions purely arbitrary? If they are arbitrary, then communication is either impossible, or very difficult.

An epistemological realism, in a broad sense, is assumed. This means that being, knowing, making, and doing are distinct but related, and that no one of them is reducible to another. It is the thesis of a phenomenological realism that this is not a view arbitrarily imposed in some a priori fashion, but rather something *found* in human experience. It repudiates as completely false the notion that what we know are our "own ideas," a view that goes back to John Locke, if not to Descartes. We can and do know our own ideas *reflexively* but *not in the first place*. The subjectivism that has vitiated modern philosophy has arisen out of such confusion. And it is this kind of subjectivism, not realism, that has made philosophical communication difficult, if not impossible. Specifically, such subjectivism does not offer an alternative thesis to, but actually eliminates the problem of, the order of teaching and learning.

With this (hopefully undogmatic) caveat in mind, we may proceed with our analysis.

In the teaching-learning activity there are three distinctions which must be made. They must be made because they are there —they are real distinctions to be discovered on analysis, and, if there is confusion in understanding them, distortions will be created in the order of teaching and learning. There are (1) the means whereby one knows; (2) the means of expressing what is known; (3) the means of teaching and learning.

The disciplines concerned with the nature of knowing are the philosophical ones called logic and epistemology (the theory of knowledge). The subject is a large and difficult one, and here it is not nor cannot be our purpose to penetrate the subtleties of the subject. It will be sufficient to clarify the nature of the subject and show its relevance to teaching.

From the standpoint of the institutional process of schooling, knowledge by acquaintance and primitive experience, though necessary, are not sufficient. Hence, the meaning of knowledge that is relevant here is that which can be both taught by the teacher and learned by the student from the teacher. Except for research work, this will be knowledge that has already been discovered by some one who "got to know." A human being knows by means of such logical instruments as concepts, propositions, and arguments (trains of reasoning). A cloudy sky may mean rain, and dog (the concept) may mean a creature of a certain kind. However, in the first case, "cloudy sky" has a structure which can be determined independently of its meaning rain; and secondly, in order to know that rain is meant, one first must know the being of a cloudy sky. The matter is different in the second case, for one first knows the creatures, dogs, and then only by a reflexive act— one which requires a great deal of intellectual sophistication—is it discovered that what dogs are is known by means of a concept and other logical entities. Furthermore, the concept of dog has no structure, i.e., no nature and no being, other than its role of *intending*. For this reason it is said that a logical entity such as concept is an "intentional" entity having mental being only.

Now, concepts are always concepts *of* something. That something may or may not exist; it may have only possible being. Hence, concepts alone may be adequate or inadequate as to *what* something is, but in themselves they are neither true nor false; for as yet there is no act of judgment; nothing has been asserted. When a judgment is made, it is by means of a proposition which has reference to existence, and not merely to essence. It is the proposition that is potentially true or false. Just as a concept has to be *of* something, a proposition has to be *about* something, and the whole nature and being of a proposition lies in its intending that which it is about. Propositions may be related in certain ways in order to get "conclusions." Whether or not the conclusions are true *because* the premises are true—this and many other questions arise in that part of logic which is called "formal."

Implicit in these distinctions is another one, that between knowing and being. In knowing *what* a dog is, I do not know my concept of dog. Dogs are spatio-temporal creatures in a real, material world. My concept is a mental entity, and nothing more, hence it does not lie out there in the real world where the dogs are. This is experimentally the case and is not a "theory." Even

Plato would admit this, for, if one insists as he did on reifying concepts, which can only be done because of a theory, then a separate realm has to be created for them. At any rate—and ours is not the metaphysical (ontological) problem—there is a difference between being a dog and the act of knowing about dogs. I do not create the being of the dogs in the act of knowing them.

The relevance of this distinction to teaching may be understood by examining the implications of its denial—in which case the teacher, in helping the students get to know what dogs are, would be in fact helping the students to make dogs; create their being. Whatever one wishes to call this, even if it were possible, it should not be called "teaching," if playing with words and sophistry is to be avoided.

At this point the voice of a critic may be heard. Does not the persuasiveness of the distinction rest upon the selection of the example? What about knowledge of ethics and of, say, religion? In the first place, the validity of the distinction is independent of the example. The example merely illustrates what is intrinsic to knowing *as such*, and not merely to a certain kind of knowing. In the second place, if the distinction is denied, then what is "taught" under the guise of ethics and religion is not knowledge; and this is admitted by those who know what they are doing. Those who do not know what they are doing can only be encouraged to find out. If the teacher in "teaching" merely helps the student to "create his own ethics," then he does this precisely because there is no knowledge to be taught. And, if so, then he is *not* teaching ethics. Nor is the matter changed by thinking of the teacher as a "guide" who brings in some kind of knowledge, namely, what people in the past have thought when they thought about ethics, this being called "resource material." What is brought in is "history," not ethics *qua* ethics. In order to get to know ethics as a systematic kind of knowledge, it is necessary to know the history of ethics; but it is not sufficient. It is one thing to introduce the students to the history of ethics because there *is* ethical knowledge, and something quite different to do it because there *is no* ethical knowledge. In the latter case, they learn not ethics, but rather past opinions that certain people had when they falsely thought that ethical knowledge exists. This is not the teaching of ethics. Teaching is a triadic relation requiring knowledge. Without knowledge of some kind, teaching is reduced to a diadic relation—in this case the determining or conditioning of the student in certain ways or in certain attitudes, especially skepticism. The student is not taught ethics, nor does he learn ethical truth. What he is taught is how to make up his "own ethics." In his ignorance of what is going on under the guise of being "educated," the student may be delighted with his task, and for reasons and motives which can easily be guessed. He either has been making or has wished he could make his own ethics.

And now the activity is sanctified by the "teacher." He is told that his new way of "education" and "teaching" is the way of the "new morality," and that it is progressive, democratic, encourages the free and open mind, etc. This is in contrast with the "old way" of teaching the ethical truth which the student learned; which way is conventional, reactionary, antidemocratic, authoritarian, and which implies a closed, dogmatic mind.

It is not at all clear exactly what the teaching of religion is, but the same principles hold. If there is no authoritative theological truth, then it cannot be taught. Hence, if "it" is "taught," then "it" is not theological truth. Rather, it is a process (activity?) whereby the "teacher" helps the "student" to create "his own conception" of "God" or gods. In recent times, the phrase "propositionless theology" has been used. Even the consistent atheist in the U.S.S.R. knows that this is not teaching, and he will have no truck with it. In fact, Lenin condemned it in a letter to Gorki as "god creating" and "god building." The reader may believe the materialist or atheist to be one hundred percent wrong; but, at least on this matter, the atheist is not confused. If there is to be teaching, then there must be some genuine, authentic theological truth to be taught. If there is no such knowledge, then there can be no teaching.

The problem we are concerned with is one on the level of teaching and learning, and not on the level of the order of knowledge. In practice, the two orders are often confused. We suggest that the matter is very clear as regards the nature of teaching and learning. If there is unclarity or confusion, it is because the problem has shifted to that of the question of whether or not there really is knowledge of the kind or kinds at issue.

If it be remarked that much of what goes on in the public schools, all the way through the State universities, in the teaching of ethics and religion is very similar to what is really nonteaching, then we can only say that the remark is a rather perceptive one, and that it defines a task for one hoping to reconstruct contemporary education.

To sum up, the distinction between being, knowing, making and doing are necessary if knowledge is possible. And, if in some certain respect the distinction between knowing and making is broken down, then in that very respect there must be a denial of knowledge. And without knowledge, there can be no teaching *in that respect*. Hence, in such a case, whatever is done under the name of teaching is not teaching. It may make ideological conditioning in one of the two ways possible, social and/or personal, or perhaps the killing of time by means of what has been called a "buzz session."

The second distinction relevant to teaching is this, that the means of expressing what is known is not the same as the means of knowing. There is a distinction between word and concept, sentence and proposition, grammar and logic. The concept, dog, may be the same in a hundred different places, yet the word standing for the concept can be different in a hundred ways. The same holds true for the other distinctions. A sentence is a unit of grammar, not of logic. Logic is concerned with the structure of thought, grammar with the structure of the language in terms of which the thought is expressed.

Since almost anything that man has ever thought of, no matter how clearly, has been denied at one time or other, so has the validity of this distinction been denied; and on one or the other of two grounds, nominalism or physicalism. Although the former does not necessarily imply the latter, in recent times they have tended to merge. Nominalism is the position that admits the reality of only singular existents, and denies the being of universal concepts. Physicalism limits all reality to the physical, hence cannot allow any place for such mental entities as concepts. Language can be allowed for, because all language-signs are physical. Now, if there is no mental being because all existents are physical, then it is easy to see how nominalism and physicalism converge. The history of the development of each, and of their convergence, is a long story and cannot be discussed here. However, a few of the implications relevant to the teaching-learning activity may be mentioned.

Nominalism implies voluntarism, the priority of the will over the intellect. This implication was serious enough for theology in the 14th century and afterwards. In fact, it was partly, but only partly, responsible for what has been called "decadent scholasticism" which, unfortunately, caused the ignorant to identify it with the whole of scholasticism. Serious enough, we suggest, for now, to put it simply but crudely, something is good because God wills it; God does not will it because it is good. Now, let us move on through history and come down to the time when it is proclaimed that "God is dead"; some kind of physicalism usually takes over, regardless of the name it goes under. The "priority of the will over the intellect" now means the priority of human interests (or the "will"?) over the intellect (or "intelligence"?). Regardless of the words that are used, what this means, in effect, is that human interests, individual and/or collective, are absolute and that intelligence must now be conceived as a mode of bodily activity. There is no longer any "intellect," there is no "will"; only the adjective "mental" can be used as modifying the physical, i.e., the intelligence becomes instrumental to the satisfying of these interests. Intellectual activity is then reduced to a kind of doing—adjusting to the environment and adjusting the environment to human interests. In fact, and quite consistently, the degree of intelligence is said to vary directly as one adjusts the environment to man. The alternative is that of being a victim of one's environment, whether it be Nature or the Social. Neither the fact nor the value of such reasoning is to be denied. What is questionable about, and in fact fatal to, this view is its inability to account for normative and theoretical reasoning.

In effect, nominalism was an ontological position which tended to negate the possibility of the ontological as a systematic discipline, in either its metaphysical or its theological forms. No room was left for any doctrine of the analogy of knowledge or of being, for terms that can be dealt with rationally are only univocal. All else is equivocation or metaphor. Mathematics and the physical sciences became models to which other kinds of knowledge should conform. The distinction between intentional and real forms vanished and logic became formalized on the model of mathematics—it being not too clear exactly what the difference was in their subject matter. There was little left for philosophers to do but analyze the physical, but now it was for the purpose of clarifying the language used by scientists who are responsible for whatever knowledge we can have. The philosophical disciplines tended to vanish from secondary education, and remained in higher education chiefly as a concession to tradition. The embarrassment of not knowing exactly what to do with philosophy was somewhat relieved by putting it on an "elective basis." The students could now choose between a course in philosophy and one in, say, Rural Sociology. All of this was rationalized under the general notion of freedom for the students—the important point being lost, of course, that freedom to get a liberal education is one thing, that freedom to determine *what* it is is another, and that the latter does not guarantee the former. But, then, if the faculty and the administration do not know, who is to say?

Even granting all of this, it may seem that there would be no implications as regards the truth about the nature of teaching, but rather only as regards the range of the truth-claims that can be taught. If so, the appearance is deceptive. If, as we have shown, philosophical knowledge is a necessity for the most effective teaching, then the nature of teaching is affected by the denial of the possibility of that kind of knowledge. Even the ethical aspects of teaching are affected. As the notion of "virtue" gives way to that of "adjustment," the notion of "pedagogy" tends to alter; for, instead of being the art of helping the students "get to know," it becomes a technique for helping them to "adjust." Students may need therapy, but such a need should not be confused with teaching or pedagogy. There is a proper meaning of "adjustment" that is quite compatible with knowing. The student is not an abstraction that the teacher teaches, and it is certainly true that in learning there is the necessity of "doing," which means "conduct." However, in a reaction against a false notion of the psychology of learning, in which the passivity of the student was overemphasized and knowledge was conceived of as something poured into his "mind," some contemporary philosophers have gone to the other extreme in so overemphasizing "doing" that its distinction from knowing tends to vanish. Neither knowing nor doing (conduct) can be a substitute for the other; rather each is instrumental to the other. But the historical effect of nominalism and physicalism has been to neglect or to deny mental being, hence the logical entities *by which* we know *what* things are—thus leaving only "doing," and the reduction of knowing to a certain kind of physical doing.

We have pointed out the importance for teaching of the distinction between the means of knowing and the means of expression, between logic and language. The third distinction is that of the means of teaching and the means of learning.

In the context of our problem, that of schooling, teaching is a kind of individual and/or institutionalized *doing* which requires various means. Knowledge is not a means of teaching, it is *what* is taught. However, there must be some means whereby such knowledge is gotten to the student. Almost anything can be a means of teaching and learning, if it proves effective and useful—blackboard, movies, chalk, etc. Most means are contingent, i.e., they may be desirable, but not absolutely necessary. The most important necessary means is the curriculum, the programming of studies. On the post-elementary levels, where a kind of knowledge is studied more systematically, this programming is referred to as a "course." A course is both a means by which the teacher teaches a kind of knowledge and the means by which the students learn. But, if a course is the same means for both teacher and student, then are not knowing and teaching the same? Since this is quite false, they must be different. But how can they be wholly different if both are means of learning, and learning is knowing?

We must distinguish meaning from manner of speaking. One cannot literally teach a course. When one so speaks he means that he teaches a course *in* mathematics or *in* physics or some other kind of knowledge. "Mathematics" is a knowledge category, "course" is a curriculum category. The teaching relation has been formalized in this way: T teaches K_1 to S. Without K_1, i.e., some kind of knowledge, teaching would be impossible. But one can, and in practice one does, say: T teaches a course *in* K_1 to S. The full implications of this may not be immediately apparent and will be more fully developed later. But a few hints may be made now. As we have said before, it is impossible to teach a course in philosophy unless there is philosophical knowledge. It is impossible to teach a course in theology unless there is that kind of knowledge. It will not help at all, because it is irrelevant, to say that what is really taught is the history of philosophy or the history of theology. How can the history of a kind of knowledge be taught if that kind of knowledge is denied? A course in the "History of Science" can be most worthwhile because there is scientific truth. Otherwise, there would be no reason to offer the course. The reason a course in the "History of Astrology" is not given is that astrology is not knowledge, whatever else it may be. To understand either philosophical or theological knowledge, the history of each is necessary but not sufficient.

A teacher can only teach a kind of knowledge, or a course *in* a kind of knowledge. The course, as a curriculum category, is *that by which* he teaches, it is not *what* he teaches. Without knowledge there can be no curriculum.

Logic is a means of *knowing*. A "course" is a means of *doing*—namely, that kind of doing which is teaching. If doing and knowing are confused, then logic and pedagogy may be confused through identification.

In order to answer another question, let us consider the curriculum, or in this case a course, from the standpoint of the student. For better or for worse, the course the student takes is the same that the teacher teaches, assuming that there is some effective teaching and learning. If the teacher *teaches* a course *in* mathematics, then the student *takes* a course *in* mathematics. The ordinary language used reflects an important distinction. We do not say that the student "learns" a course in mathematics. He *learns* mathematics, but *takes* the course.

And now to the question: What is the purpose of the course as a curricular instrument? It is to help the student learn mathematics, to get to know mathematics. But was not the point just made that logic is an instrument of knowing, that a course is an instrument of teaching, and that the two are quite different? A "curriculum" is not "logic."

The answer lies in recognizing that the phrase "means of knowing" can mean two quite different things, the one logical and the other psychological. We say a student learns about the structure of matter by means of the scientific method, the study of which method is a part of logic. Whether he reflectively studies the method or not, the student gets to know, learns about, the structure of matter by means of certain logical methods. But we can also say that the student learned through a course in chemistry. Logic is a means of knowing and learning *by which* there is an intellectual assimiliation of the truth. A curricular entity such as a course is that *by means of which* the student through the teacher gets to know, learns some kind of knowledge *by means of* logical methods. The first "by means of" is psychological and/or social, the latter "by means of" is logical.

The student is a human being with feelings and emotions, with will and interests. He is not a logical machine which can be programmed like a computer. In teaching a computer what to do, one does not have to worry about psychological or social problems that the computer may have. But the student, whatever else he may be, is at least a psycho-social being. The problem is how to get a kind of knowledge, the nature and structure of which is just what it is independent of the psychological, *into* the mind of the student. If one is teaching mathematics, there is nothing in the nature of that subject to tell one how to get the student to learn it.

A curriculum, then, which is a means of teaching and learning is a synthesis that has two necessary constituents—knowledge of one or more kinds to be taught, on the one hand, and pedagogical techniques based on the psycho-social knowledge of students, on the other. An example on the elementary level may illustrate. Manipulation of apples has nothing whatsoever to do with the nature of mathematics as knowledge. It is not a means of proving anything in mathematics. But it can be part of a pedagogical technique (however old-fashioned!) by means of which the teacher teaches mathematics to the student. Both the manipulation of the apples, as part of the curricular plan, and the teacher himself are part of the total complex of efficient causes by which the student learns. But mathematical knowledge is the formal cause.

Whether or not the manipulation of apples is a good way to teach about numbers is not the issue at all. There may be better ways. The point is that good teaching must take into account the psychological as well as the logical, and that it is partly the function of pedagogy to do this. If the teacher came into the classroom and announced that the students are to learn about the cardinal numbers, and then proceed in the manner of Vol. I of *Principia Mathematica* of Whitehead and Russell, or in some other similar manner, then the students would probably soon be throwing paper wads at each other. With apples, it is different. They taste good! This does not at all prove that the "new-mathematics" is not necessary. What is questionable is whether it is pedagogically sufficient.

If all this may seem somewhat obvious to the pedagogical sophisticate, it has not always been so, and in schools of education the full implications of the distinctions have not as yet been reflected in programs for the preparation of teachers. In the United States at least, departments of education have tended to require of their students, who become our future teachers, that they study the "psychology of education"; which is all well and good. But the same have been woefully deficient in requiring these students to understand the nature of knowledge, the order of knowledge, the logical (and philosophical) basis of the special subjects they are to teach. In short, the means of knowing and the means of teaching have often become confused, with the result that the former has suffered in teacher-education programs. Of course, this means that in the long run the latter suffers also.

THE NATURE OF TRUTH

A kind of knowledge consists of an organized group of propositions for which truth-claims are made. It is not necessary that every truth-claim be true. Human knowledge is never that perfect. It is necessary, however, that not every truth-claim be false. This is simply to say, in an indirect way, that man is man and is neither

Knowledge as the Formal Cause in Teaching and Learning

God nor beast. If there is no truth, there can be no knowledge and no teaching. A brief analysis of the nature of truth will be sufficient if we show not only what it is, but also what it must be, in some minimal sense in order that teaching and learning may be possible.

Truth and falsity are attributed to propositions. Concepts are adequate or inadequate, and arguments are valid or invalid. With respect to truth and falsity, a proposition has fundamental relations to its referent, i.e., what the proposition is *about*, and to the mental act of the person who makes the judgment.

A sentence may or may not express a proposition; but, if it does, then the proposition must be *about* something, must have a referent, just as a concept must be *of* something. It is through these that existence and essences can be known, and as intentional signs their whole being lies in intending such. Propositions are always about something other than themselves, except when, reflexively as in logic, propositions are themselves studied. At any rate, whether one talks of man, nature, or God, propositions are not "out there" with the referents. Propositions are mental beings, and are purely human creations.

Does this mean that man also creates truth? No, for "truth" and "proposition" are not synonyms. A proposition may be true or false; yet it is still a proposition, and its being false does not make it less so. In short, what makes for the being of a proposition is not identical with that which makes for the being of its truth. What makes for the being of the truth-relation is its conformity, relatively or absolutely, to its referent. To understand the exact nature of this relation of conformity—or, in the case of falsity, nonconfromity—one would have to turn to epistemology. It will suffice for our purpose merely to identify the being of the truth-relation, and then to show its implications for the order of teaching and learning.

A proposition also has a relation to the mind of the person, and in two ways. A mental act created the proposition. Second, by a mental act of judgment, one may assert the truth or falsity of it. Sometimes a "proposition" and a "judgment" are identified. It is true that for some purposes the distinction is not relevant. But we would call attention to the fact that a person can create a proposition and not make a judgment of its truth or falsity. He may merely find it interesting and toy with it, withholding judgment. Furthermore, responsibility for a knowledge-claim does not come with the creation of a proposition, but with its assertion or denial in believing or disbelieving it. I have made a *correct* judgment if it is in accordance with the *being* of the truth-relation. Otherwise, it is incorrect, relatively or absolutely. The qualification is necessary in order to recognize that there are degrees of knowledge and, properly interpreted, degrees of truth. Absolute truth and absolute falsity are the two ends of the knowledge spectrum. Most of man's knowledge falls in between, this being reflected in the language we use, e.g., "highly probable," "plausible," "somewhat doubtful."

It is not the case, as some have thought, that a qualification destroys the truth-relation by dissolving it into some kind of subjective relativity. There are many kinds of knowledge, hence different modes and degrees of truth. But, unless the nature of the truth-relation can be understood and identified, there would be nothing which one could speak of as a degree or mode. The qualification also implies a rather subtle distinction between the "being of truth" and the "knowing of truth." The epistemologist knows the difficulty, both systematic and historical, of trying to bring the two together. However, if the distinction is denied, one's difficulties are multiplied a hundred-fold, as the history of modern philosophy shows.

For our purpose, an example may sufficiently illustrate. Let us suppose that I assert, at the time of this writing, that Hitler is dead. Is my judgment correct or incorrect? Is it or is it not true? The two questions are not identical. For there is an existential issue here, quite independent of the question of adequacy of concepts—which would be an issue on the level of essence. Hitler is either dead or alive. It is a matter of "either-or, but not both." Hence, from the standpoint of the *being* of truth I can say that my proposition is either absolutely true or absolutely false. There are no 'degrees." But, from the standpoint of my *knowing* the truth, the matter is somewhat different. When I say that I know that Hitler is dead, my knowledge-claim is functionally related to the quantity and quality of evidence. Hence, although from the standpoint of the being of the truth, "Hitler is dead," if true, is an absolutely true proposition, nevertheless from the standpoint of knowing one must say that it is highly plausible that the proposition is true—in fact, so much so that the burden of proof would fall on the person who would question it.

If a true proposition had no foundation "in the nature of things," had no being distinct, though not separable, from the act of knowing, then there could be no degrees of knowing. The qualifications "not separable" is important. Although for the purpose of analysis the distinction is *there*, from the standpoint of the whole *act of knowing* the proposition and the judgment merge together, and then the truth-relation is said to be bi-polar. At one end of the relation is the "thing" known, the referent, which is independent of the act of knowing so far as its being is concerned. At the other end is the knowing mind, the mental act of knowing. Eliminate either end and truth is impossible. It is for this reason that it can equally be said that truth is subjective or that truth is objective. Without persons with "minds," who have private, subjective natures, there could be no truth. But it is the function of the "mental" to discover, not to create, truth. What is created are the propositions, not their truth or falsity. To absolutize the subjective end of the relation is to make an "ism out of it—subjectivism, which, because of its denial of one end of the truth-relation, makes truth impossible.

Equally, it can be said that truth is static, unchanging, and also that it is dynamic and "becoming." Perhaps nothing could be more static or unchanging than the *being* of the truth or the falsity, whichever it is, of the proposition that Hitler is now dead. However, the act of knowing it is dynamic, and the knowing of its truth "becomes" with the accumulation of evidence. There are other ways of expressing this. It can be said from the standpoint of the being of truth that a proposition is actually true, but, from the standpoint of the knowing of the truth, assuming that it is not as yet known, that the proposition is only potentially true. It is through the activity of knowing that such potentiality becomes actual. What was actually true in the being of a proposition is now actually true in the knowing of the truth, i.e., to the degree there is a conformity of "mind" to "thing"; and this is what one seeks if one seriously seeks the truth.

In teaching and learning, truth must be taught and learned. Except for the higher levels of research, the purpose of the teacher is to teach different kinds of knowledge—different modes of truth—that have already been discovered. The student, in learning, gets to know these truths. However, the student's "getting to know" is not necessarily the same as the "getting to know" of the person or persons who first discovered the truth the student is learning. Especially is this true in the elementary grades. In the first few years, the student is presented mathematics which, in the history of man, took centuries or longer to develop. The student neither does, nor can, literally repeat the knowing activity of the discoverers of the knowledge. And this is the case for any kind of knowledge, not just mathematics.

The difference in the two activities of "getting to know" may be expressed in this way: *The student rediscovers the truth someone else has discovered.* It is the function of the teacher to help the student make this rediscovery. This teaching-learning activity is not possible if there are no true propositions; the being of the truth having a reality independent of the minds of both teacher and student. It is not just a corruption of teaching to speak of the teacher creating truth or helping the student to do so. Rather, it is a total denial of teaching, reducing it to a diadic relation.

Only on the higher levels or research does the student become a discoverer of new truth. But, precisely because it is new, the student cannot learn it in the manner in which he has been learning all of his life. For the same reason the teacher cannot teach it to him. What the teacher can teach the student is how to discover new truth. However, this teaching now is about the logic of research methods in a particular field of knowledge; it is not directly the teaching of that field itself. The student learns this because he has prepared himself for it by spending years "mastering his subject" through rediscovering what others had long ago discovered. Thus, he merits the right to transcend the knowledge he has been taught.

At this point someone may say that this is a most "conservative," in fact "reactionary," view of teaching and learning. It leaves no room for creativity, it is not "modern," it cannot meet the educational needs of a dynamic "contemporary" society, etc. A little analysis will show that at minimum there has been a misunderstanding, and at most an emotional reaction expressed through the use of certain words in their ideological meanings.

First, to speak in generalities. *Not only* is creativity a desirable human quality, it is absolutely necessary to perfect oneself as a human being. Who would disagree? Certainly not a materialist, naturalist, or secularist. They insist upon it. Not the theologian, at the other end of the ontological spectrum; for man, created in the image of God, is and must be creative *because* God is creative. What, then, is the problem? The problem is that of the correct *locus* of creativity. Confining ourselves still to the realm of generalities, hence, in a sense, of vagaries, let us remember that Hitler, Al Capone, Jesus Christ, St. Thomas Aquinas, St. Francis, the Devil, and God were (are) all creative in some sense or other. It is the "sense" that matters, and to analyze that we must become more specific.

The sharpness of the distinctions we have made need not be carried over with equal sharpness to the temporal process of education. As we have already seen, in his movement up the educational ladder, the student gradually proceeds from knowing *that* to knowing *why*. In the history of the physical sciences, each new insight, each new truth discovered, represents a creative action to some extent. After all, any new truth has to be expressed in a proposition, and that proposition—not the truth—had to be newly created by a scientific worker. The scientist may be said to be creative in his imagination and thinking. The meaning of such creativity may be passed on to the student by having him repeat the experimental activity of the original discoverer. In this way, the student may learn how later to be an original discoverer himself. This is creative learning, and it may be illustrated in the following way.

In a course of physics, the student may be handed an equation expressing a physical "law." With experimental apparatus, the student learns how to use it and, interestingly enough, if he follows directions carefully, it always "works." He gets the "right answers." After proceeding this way a sufficient number of times, he finds that he gets a good grade in the course. Furthermore, he has acquired knowledge he can later use in engineering. What has he learned? He has learned *that*, but not *why*. How was the formula obtained in the first place? This he has not learned. Neither the learning nor the teaching has been as yet creative.

The equation containing the law has a locus, a curve. How were the curve and the equation obtained? The experimental data acquired are represented by dots. Can a curve be run through all of these dots, or through just some of them? If the latter, which "some" are to fall on the curve, and which are to fall off? And so on. Why this curve rather than that? In the back of the student's text on analytical geometry there may be a chapter on "curve-fitting." But the chances are that, because of the pressure of time, it is the chapter left out of the course. But the student should learn how to "fit" curves, if he wants to understand the "why." The singular bits of data acquired through experimental procedure do not automatically give one the universal formula which can order them. The trick is to *discover* the pattern of order exemplified in the data. When the student learns how the originator did it, and then duplicates the experiment, he knows *why* the formula works, and not merely *that* it does.

It may be granted that much of learning will be confined to the "that." It is a question of time. There simply isn't enough time to duplicate all of the creative procedures by which new truths have been discovered. But the student should be acquainted with selected examples sufficient to enable him to understand what creative imagination and thinking really are.

In what sense should the teacher and the student *not* be creative? Creative teaching is effectively helping the student to learn creatively. Because of his superior knowledge and maturity, the teacher will also guide the student in making appraisals as to what truth is important and what is not. The *being* of truth alone does not confer importance. A student could become very creative and count the number of leaves on the tree outside the classroom window. Not only will he have discovered a new truth, but he will also be the only person in the history of mankind to possess it! It is the duty of a creative teacher to prevent such "creative" learning.

A false kind of creative teaching is often to be found in the encouragement of students "to make up their own ideas and opinions." Since any idea or opinion has to belong to someone, if a student has an idea or opinion, it can be said that it is his idea or opinion. If a student's opinion is true, it is his opinion. If a student's opinion is false, it is his opinion. Now what is important is whether or not the opinion is true or false. The fact that he has an opinion is irrelevant to this question, for it will still be "his" opinion whether it be true or false. The teacher should prevent such creativity and explain the reason to the student—that creativity is wonderful if correctly expressed, that he hopes the student will, through a rediscovery of old truth, sufficiently master the subject at hand that he can later merit the right to be creative in the discovery of new truth.

It is not so much in mathematics and the physical sciences as in "social" subjects that such antiteaching is to be found. For example, a teacher may have students write a little essay on "What democracy means to me." In abstraction from further information, this could be either good or bad. It is bad if the teacher does not give them knowledge about democracy, explain *what* democracy is, for otherwise the essay becomes a subjective substitute for truth. In so far as the student learns anything at all, it is that about such a matter there is no knowledge, only subjective opinions—"So here is mine; this is the way I feel about it."

Truth is grasped in the act of *knowing*; teaching is a kind of *doing*. Creative teaching is helping the student grasp the truth. For either the teacher or the student deliberately to talk of creating truth is the beginning of the corruption of the teaching-learning activity. Actually to attempt to do it is antiteaching and antilearning. Relative to the nature of truth, what is created is the language which expresses it, and the concepts, propositions, and arguments by means of which it is grasped. But whether or not a concept is adequate, a proposition is true, or an argument is valid depends upon the nature of the reality intended and not upon the free, creative act of intending. If this were not so, then in the act of knowing one would have to create the reality one professes to know, and in the act of teaching one would be helping the student to "make the world." The making and remaking that constitutes individual and social action can be good, but only when it is based upon truth and not upon a substitute for it.

Modern subjectivism has, unfortunately, crept into educational practice, usually in the nontechnical and nonscientific areas, and the effect is the contemporary confusion to which reference has been made many times. The age which has given us the "antihero" has also given us the "antistudent" and the "antiteacher."

We may remember that our hypothetical critic raised the question of "creativity" in connection with our view of teaching and learning, with the implication that the position taken is reactionary and unprogressive. Perhaps we have now merited the right to deny the implication, for we have shown by analysis that there is no question of creativity in the abstract, that the only thing to be objected to is the giving of a false locus to creative action, and that if this is not avoided the error is a subjectivism which renders teaching impossible. However, there is more to be said.

The *order* of teaching and learning has nothing whatever to do with such terms as "progressive," "conservative," or "reactionary." Nor is it a "view," except in the sense of a truism. There is only one kind of criticism of our analysis that is relevant, that in some way or other it is false or inadequate. The order of teaching and learning is what it is. The order of the heavenly bodies is just what it is. The anatomical order of the human being is just what it is. The only problem in all of these is to state as accurately as possible what the orders are. Every statement on these orders is a "view" in the sense that some one has to "view" them. But such a truism is not very helpful. The relevant issue is one of truth and falsity, and we can only hope that whatever is false or inadequate in our analysis will be pointed out by someone, or that someone may perfect this analysis.

It may be said that something has been overlooked in our comparison of the order of teaching and learning with physical orders, namely that the question of ends, norms, values does not arise in the description of physical orders. With teaching and learning, it is different. Given one set of values, a certain theory of teaching and learning logically (formally) follows; postulate another set of values, and a different "view" follows. Hence, there is no such thing as *the* order of teaching and learning; there are only different views, each of which might prove useful at different times and places, and under different social conditions.

Now, of course, there is a difference between physical orders and the order of teaching and learning. But because there is a difference it does not necessarily follow from that fact alone that there can be no knowledge of values. The critic is assuming a doctrinal skepticism as regards values, ends, and norms of education, and then deduces that there can be no order of teaching and learning. But this is to beg the question; it is assuming what needs to be demonstrated.

Secondly, such criticism has nothing to do with the question of the truth or falsity of our analysis of the order of teaching and learning. Rather, as a doctrinal skepticism it is a thesis on the level of epistemology, and as such denies the *possibility* of any knowledge about the order of teaching and learning. In fact, it makes teaching itself impossible. If there is no truth in the objective sense we have defined, or in some other more adequate sense, then obviously there is no truth about the order of teaching and learning.

Even if skepticism takes a more limited form, which it usually does in order not to be self-contradictory, still the matter is not changed in any essential respect. In such a case, the argument is this: there is the order of teaching and learning as we have described, but it is limited to *what* can be taught—as we have so insistently stated. Now what can be taught is that which is knowledge, and there is no objective truth about values, ethics, all knowledge being limited to mathematics, history, and the positive sciences. This is positivism, of course; but again the thesis is on the level of epistemology. It is a thesis about the limited nature of knowledge and truth; it is not another "view," in contrast with our analysis, of the order of teaching and learning.

Positivism would seem at least to leave room for our analysis of the order of teaching and learning, even though in an emaciated form. The appearance is deceptive. The most serious reason for rejecting the positivistic criticism—in fact a fatal one—is that positivism, if it makes a knowledge-claim, represents a kind of knowledge not allowed for by positivism itself. A self-contradictory position can hardly give an alternative view, not even a limited one, of the order of teaching and learning, for it cannot deal responsibly with the problem of the ends and values of education, liberal or otherwise. On the other hand, if positivism—or any other similar position, for the name is not important—makes no knowledge-claim, then it is simply an ideology which has a *use function* in the war against philosophical and theological truth. If the schools and the teachers in them create attitudes in students against the possibility of metaphysical, theological, and ethical truth, then that school is "progressive" and not "old-fashioned," etc.

This is intellectual violence, war, and makes intelligent communication impossible. One cannot refute ideology in terms of evidence or truth, for it has only *use* values. The most one can do intellectually is simply show what it is.

To sum up thus far, we have tried to state in brief form the minimal meaning of truth presupposed in teaching and learning, and the locus of creativity in such activities. In this attempt, we have tried to describe phenomenologically *what is there*, what is, in part, intrinsic to the essential *nature* of teaching-learning. This is the complete opposite from starting with a pattern of ideas, a "theory," a pattern or order, and then *imposing* it upon the teaching-learning activity. Since this is literally impossible anyway, what in fact is done is that from this formal order, the formal postulates (which are postulated because of their functional value, their use value), it is then deduced what teaching *must* be as an activity in order that it will serve these use values.

In this ideological approach, it *can* be said that there are different "views" of "teaching" and "learning." The reason is that the whole matter is now put on the level of "means," hence one means, i.e., one "view," is "better" perhaps than another. However, even in giving this exposition it was necessary for accuracy to put teaching and learning in quotation marks. For reference cannot be to these activities in their objective, ordered relation; rather reference *can only be to the use-function of the words.*

The final sophistry is simply, by an arbitrary act, to reverse the causality on "use" and "truth." Instead of a proposition being useful because it is true, it is now said that it is true because it is useful. The twentieth century has been witness to the implications in practice of this kind of pragmatism. But time moves on, and so during the latter part of the century the technique has been for the sophisticated ideologist to put even the term "truth" in quotation marks, meaning of course "truth" other than in the positive sciences. Others, recognizing the philosophical schizophrenia of past positivism, would go further and consistently deny any "truth" that is not man-made.

Any truth-claim made about the order of teaching and learning presupposes the *being* of truth. And so does any criticism of the truth-claim, and which makes such criticism possible as relevant and welcome. Also relevant and welcome is an alternative presentation ("view") of the order of teaching and learning that is more adequate and "truer." All this presumes intelligent communication, and is implied in the notion of "a community of scholars." What is unfortunate is the ideological and antiintellectualistic approach of so many educators and administrators who reject the implications of an order of teaching and learning because, to put it crudely but bluntly as one administrator did, "they don't serve my purpose."

PROPOSITIONS, INTERESTS, AND IDEOLOGY

In the bi-polar truth relation, we have seen that one pole is the knower himself. A person, however, is much more than a knower, for he has feelings and emotions, interests and purposes, of many kinds. The person also has two fundamental natural relations, the one a relation of self-identity to his whole past development, and the other constituted by his social relations. Sometimes these relations are confused with the knowing relation, much to the detriment of the latter, thus making possible the antiintellectualism of ideological thinking, and with consequent unfortunate effects in teaching and learning.

A person has a history, as Freud and others have so correctly insisted when criticizing both behaviorism and sensationism in psychology. As such, far from being some kind of abstract, conscious knower, a person is a bundle of drives and interests, most of which he may not be conscious of or understand. Hence, a distinction must be made between the interest an individual actually acts on and the interest he gives consciously as the "reason" for his action. To assume that they are always the same is simply factually false, an assumption that characterizes certain extreme forms of rationalism. In effect, it is to make an "ism" out of the intellectual aspect of man, and such intellectual*ism* allows no room for the nonrational and irrational which constitutes much of human behavior.

Although Freud and his followers emphasized the function of the sex drive in explaining human behavior, to understand the truth of his position and to make use of it for our purpose, it is not necessary to stress the questionableness of such emphasis. An example may be helpful. Let us suppose that a student is arguing against the extension of the military draft. He marshals his evidence very persuasively, pointing out that the immediate conditions which made such an extension plausible, following the Korean war, no longer exist, that the draft wastes many of the important years of a young man's life, etc. Now, the *real* reason may be quite different from the ones consciously expressed. In this case, it may be pointed out that the student is really rebelling against an authoritarian father whom he felt made him suffer as a child, that the draft represents a step toward an authoritarian state, or at least the danger of it, etc. The student is not aware of the different sets of reasons, yet the real reasons are not the ones consciously given. The ones consciously given are, therefore, "rationalizations" covering up real motivations.

That such rationalizations do occur is certainly true. In fact Freud, in some respects, was recapturing old truths that had been lost because of the effect of Cartesianism on the development of psychology. It may be granted, therefore, that Freudian psychology was a healthy emphasis against the naivete of the older psychology. Had that been the end of the matter, there would be no need of mentioning it here. But this was not the case. Implicit in Freud, and more explicit in some of his followers, was a tendency to absolutize these psychological insights. Psychology alone cannot absolutize itself. It can only be done on "philosophical" grounds, even though there be no philosophical evidence to support it. At any rate, when done, certain implications follow, e.g., the primacy of the nonrational over the rational as an a priori postulate in terms of which all human actions are to be understood and interpreted, and not merely as a psychological description of how, so often, people do act.

One may well imagine what can happen; and it has in fact happened in educational theory and practice. Theological statements become projections of insecure people who, having left the warmth of the home where there was a real father, now attempt to recapture that warmth and security by believing in a big "Papa" in the sky. The philosophical disciplines tend to be reduced to rationalizations which are personal ideologies or *Weltanschauungs,* and about which philosophers endlessly and uselessly quarrel, on the naive assumption that on such matters there is some kind of evidence to which a rational appeal can be made.

If, on all levels of education, philosophical knowledge is required on the part of the teacher and if such knowledge is not merely absent but literally impossible, then the teaching activity suffers as well as the learning activity of the student. There is nothing wrong in a word or phrase as such, and certainly the term "mental hygiene" is innocent. However, objection can be made to some things that go on under that name. For often the student is handed, under the guise of psychology, a few psychological facts and insights mixed with a good many deductions from a naturalistic philosophy, it all being dignified by calling it a "scientific approach." In some cases, the student becomes almost a "patient" and the teacher a "therapist" in some amateur manner. If this does not work out well with individual teachers who are trying to teach some kind of knowledge to students, than counselors are brought in. There is nothing wrong with the word "counselor." Nor is there any objection to "vocational counseling." But the matter is somewhat different when this "trained" counselor, not knowing the difference between psychology and philosophy and theology, attempts to guide little girls in sex matters. What is overlooked is the pridefulness attached to such amateurish, third-rate "teaching" about some of the most important matters of life.

It is good mental hygiene to recognize that the student is not a "pure intellect" that only assimilates knowledge in some degree proportional to the pedagogical art of the teacher. Hence, a student may require the attention of those who can help him as a *person,* and not just as a "knower." But it is a mark of wisdom for each institution to know its limitations. Otherwise, it cannot know even its essential function. The purpose of the school is to see that the teacher teaches truth, in so far as it is known, and that the student learns it. It is not a place where the teacher has a right to pass off as knowledge his own ignorance, his personal "philosophy of life," his own ideology. Nor is the school's primary function to be a substitute for a hospital or a church. If this is overlooked or forgotten, then again, as we have mentioned so often, there is a tendency to reduce the teaching relation to a diadic one. The student is "adjusted," "determined," "indoctrinated" on a sub-intellectual level, without ever really knowing what is happening to him.

The reduction of all philosophical and theological knowledge to personal ideology is not merely false from the standpoint of the order of knowledge—for it confuses philosophy and psychology—but it is also self-contradictory, hence literally nonsense. Everyone can "get into the act," and any appeal to evidence can be dismissed as a "rationalization." But, of course, this must apply to the "Freudian" himself. Following the materialistic "philosophy" of the followers of Freud—not his valuable psychological insights—the so-called Freudian must exempt himself from his own principles—for he must hold that his thesis is true in the real sense, and is not itself an ideology, a personal *Weltanschauung*, a "feeling," a "personal opinion," etc. This is to say in effect that the "philosophy," and not only the psychology, of Freud means that it is "rational" to believe that most, if not all, "rational" activities of human beings are irrational; not merely *de facto*—in which case the Freudian psychologist has a point—but rather that a priori, they *cannot* be rational, that there is literally no question of evidence.

A person not only has a personal history, psychologically speaking, but also exists in a social context. If psychological relations have sometimes been confused with the knowing relation, so has it been the case that some have made a similar confusion of the social relations with the knowing relation. If the name of Freud can be identified with the former, the name of Marx can be associated with the latter.

Freud emphasized sex, Marx the notion of class. The term "class" has a specific meaning in Marxism. Ultimately, one's "class character" is determined by one's relations to "property in the means of production." If a person owned such property or helped to manage such property, he would think in a certain way. On the other hand, if a person is a "worker," having nothing to sell but his "labor-power," then he will think in another way. In other words, a person's "mind" is a reflection of the material conditions in which he lives. For example, because the southern, white bourgeoise in the United States are landowners, small business men, or have a class-status because of their relation to such propertied people, they hold certain beliefs about Negroes. On the other hand, the Negroes have different beliefs about both themselves and the white people because they are the victims of exploitation and discrimination.

It may be granted that "up to a point" this is true. The qualification, "up to a point," is necessary because of a lurking ambiguity in such a simple presentation. Had Marx and his followers been satisfied with calling attention to the *fact* that, under the guise of truth-claiming, many people merely reflect their wants and wishes, economic and otherwise, then they would have joined a group of scholars, both religious and secular, down through the ages who have also called attention to the egotism and pridefulness of man in his social relations. But such is not the essence of Marxism—that which uniquely defines it.

The essential nature of Marxism lies not in the facts to be explained, but in the explanation of the facts. For they must be understood in terms of "dialectical materialism," a position assumed rather than argued for—the reason being that the time has come to change the world, as Marx said, rather than to endlessly debate ontological interpretations of it, as do the bourgeoise. Hence, the Marxist argues *from* materialism, and, when he does so, what is a fact that may be recognized by anyone with goodwill now becomes an ontological necessity. This means that a person, in his being as a knower, not merely does, or may, reflect his class position, but *must* do so. (Even the case of the capitalist who becomes a communist is "explained" in terms of the materialist dialectic.) By an intellectual act, and through an act of goodwill, it is impossible for a person to grasp the *being* of truth *in spite* of his material relations, physical or social.

The issue here is not whether the "material" is necessary. It is, for man, whatever else he may be, is at least a material creature. But, for material*ism*, what is necessary is here also sufficient. As a consequence there is confusion between the reason for the *being* of the truth of a proposition and the reason *why* a person may believe the proposition.

If a person were absolutely perfect and could never believe anything else, then the two reasons would become one. The only reason why a person would believe a proposition would be *because* in its *being* it is true. Now this is the perfection of the Deity, and undoubtedly as an ideal and as a norm it practically defines rationality. For a given person, it means that, regardless of his class relations by virtue of being a wealthy owner of property in the means of production, there should never be a conflict between the two reasons. And, if a potential conflict tends to become actual, then it is resolved immediately by the person by changing his class relations and all beliefs about them to conform to truth. Such perfection is, of course, not descriptive of what any person consistently does; nor is it possible for a human being to be so consistent. It is a counsel of perfection always to try to have the two reasons the same. This is what it means to be a "truth-seeker." Although there is only one reason why a proposition is true, namely, its conformity to its referent, and although it is a counsel of perfection to have that same reason as the only one explaining *why* it is believed, nevertheless, because man is man and not God, both the possibility and the actuality (in some cases) of the two reasons not being the same must be admitted. A person may, *because* of his class status, his social relations, believe something that is quite false. The "social" explains why a false proposition is believed, but it does not and cannot be the reason why the proposition is false.

Now, if it is a most serious error for man implicitly to deify himself by *reducing* the "why I believe" to the "why a proposition is true," it is an equal error to reduce the "why a proposition in its being is true or false" to "why a person believes the proposition to be true or false." It is this converse that may be identified with Marxism. Why does Ivan not have the right to a higher education? Because his father was a capitalist. From the standpoint of truth, what would be relevant would be the question of the natural right

Knowledge as the Formal Cause in Teaching and Learning 111

of the student *as a person*. But no, it is a "class matter," and "truth" is determined accordingly.

Again, and referring not to the present but to the earlier history of the Soviet Union, consider the proposition, "Jesus never lived." Why is this proposition true? It is a proposition concerned with history, and one might think that it was a matter of evidence, the kind sought for by the historian disciplined in historiography. No, the reason *why* it is true is that it is the contradictory of the proposition, "Jesus lived," which is false. Why is it false? Because it was a belief created by class exploiters to hold down the masses.

Here we have, again, the ideological determination of "truth." Since this is actually impossible, the word must be put in quotation marks. Instead of trying, through the proper kind of education, to base the philosophical disciplines and social sciences on the being of truth—which, as we have seen is a counsel of perfection, but also the meaning of rationality and goodwill in the seeking of truth—the whole process is inverted. The philosophical and the social subjects are reduced to the ideological, from which "truth" is deduced, the ideological ultimately being a pattern of ideas of a future social order to be progressively approached.

In so far as this is put into educational practice—and Marxists have never been wholly consistent in doing this—then truth, being ideologically determined, renders knowledge impossible (wherever it occurs), and teaching is reduced from a triadic to a diadic relation. For the student is "conditioned," and that relation is a diadic one.

At this point, a note should be made of something far too important to be buried in a footnote, for otherwise there may be a misunderstanding in connection with the example we have used, Marxism, and which may be carried over to throw doubt upon the principles the example was supposed to exemplify. The careful student of Marxism may be quick to point out that the notion of Marxism we have presented is a complete distortion, the whole purpose of dialectical materialism being to give a realistic basis for social relations; that we have confused Utopian socialism and Scientific socialism; that we have confused ideology in the romantic, utopian fashion with ideology in its *scientific* form; and that the very *being* of Marxism is, in its essence, the negation of the formalism and subjectivism of which we have accused it, etc.

Contrary to what the critic might suspect, in a Judo-like fashion we shall recognize some truth to this criticism. The point is, we are not doubting so much the truth as the relevance of what he says. And the reason is this. What the critic is doing is pointing out the other side of the story, that once having attained power through the 1917 revolution the Marxists found that, to come to grips with existential realities, ideology, even if called "scientific," is not only not sufficient but can be obstructive. Interestingly enough, where dialectical materialism first had to be given up was in the physical sciences themselves. On paper the Einstein theory could be condemned as "bourgeois physics," but, if an industrial complex and military hardware are to be developed, then so much the worse for ideology. The Nazis had already called the Einstein theory "Jewish physics." Whether or not class or race is emphasized, the one ideological interpretation is just as false or nonsensical as the other.

In biology, there has also been an ideological struggle in the U.S.S.R. between the dialectical materialists and those who insisted upon the experimental method which defines it as scientific in the nonideological sense. The "dialectic" is an ontological category and, with the implication of an extreme theory of "internal relations," it was deduced that Mendelian genetics, with its denial of the inheritance of acquired characteristics, was nondialetical, which, of course, it is. Lysenko and other biologists, backed by the government ideologists, proceeded accordingly in the growing of grain. But the Soviet people had to eat, or at least it was preferable to reading ideological essays which are not very nourishing physically. Thus, over time, Lysenko and the ideologists fell out of favor.

In short, if people are to eat and to develop the industrial and the military, then the *being* of truth about Nature must be grasped and accepted as opposed to the ideological approach which *imposes* ideas on Nature. But this necessitated a corresponding change on the level of teaching and learning, and so the "progressive education" introduced in the nineteen twenties, and attributed to the followers of John Dewey, was gradually given up in the teaching of mathematics and the positive sciences. For students had to learn the truth about Nature, and the teachers had to teach it. There was the urgency of time. As the ideological approach was gradually given up, a great deal of progress was made, with the result that in the second half of the twentieth century, the non-Communist world paid attention to the contributions of the Soviet scientists, especially the mathematicians.

Has, then, all ideology been eliminated in the schools of the U.S.S.R.? By no means. A non-Marxist might feel quite at home in a Soviet classroom in physics or chemistry. But, the moment he steps into a classroom in literature, philosophy, history, or social science, he enters into an infinitely different world, for here ideology with but a few exceptions still reigns supreme. However, the bright student is increasingly asking embarrassing questions about the "meaning of life," the moral and spiritual nature of man. He grows restless under Party slogans, and vaguely suspects that there is truth transcending the ideology of the Party, truth in terms of which not only the day-by-day decisions of the Party may be judged, but even Marxism itself. The *ad hoc* rationalizations of the meaning of human existence in terms of ideology are no longer sufficient. Not true science, but the use of the term as an ideological weapon, is being challanged by some who dare the risk. The Party orthodox are quite aware of all of this; furthermore they realize that if the trend continues it means ultimately the death of Marxism and Communism *in essence*, even though the names may be retained.

All of this is in reply to the critic who might suggest, as noted previously, that we distorted Marxism. We are sympathetic with the reasons why he might say it and, as we have said before, we may admit an element of truth in it. But it does not change anything essentially in regard to our analysis of the order of teaching and learning. All it means is that the Marxists themselves have major, not minor, problems, and that no one can accuse a Marxist of the distortion of Marxism as much, and as effectively, as another Marxist. This is part of the ideological history of the Soviet Union. As regards relevancy to the problem we were dealing with, the point is this: to the degree Marxism retains its ideological character there is a breakdown of the order of teaching and learning, and that to the degree it is not retained, Marxism vanishes.

In their ideological character, both Marxism and Freudianism are examples of what has been called the "genetic fallacy." It is the error of supposing that the historical, social, or psychological origin of a belief determines its truth or falsity. "John Jones says X is Y, and I know it is false." "Why?" "Because the man is crazy." Now, the being of the truth or falsity of the proposition in question is not determined by Jones' mental condition. A crazy person may say something that is true or something that is false. However, the truth or falsity is quite independent of the fact that he says it. The mental condition of a man may be relevant in explaining why he believes a proposition that is false, if on independent grounds there is evidence that it is false.

The genetic fallacy is by no means limited to Freudianism or Marxism. The ideological use of terms is quite common to some teachers, journalists, and others who are quite innocent of any real knowledge of such terms. The effect on the learning activity is disastrous. A student may neither be encouraged nor allowed to study systematically ethics or theology, and yet teachers may assert as true or condemn as false a hundred and one propositions having to do with man's moral and spiritual life, the student learning little more than that the "good" is contemporary, new, and modern, while the "bad" is conventional, traditional, or old-fashioned. Such subintellectual ideological indoctrination is not teaching at all; it is antiteaching. The moral and spiritual lives of students are, of course, adversely affected, much to the consternation—and here is the irony—of those who defend such a perversion under the name of "freedom of teaching."

There is the possibility of a misunderstanding at this point, and it must be avoided. Are we maintaining that, under the notion of teaching, what is traditional in ethics and religion must be taught? And that, if someone advocates a change in any respect—and are not all changes contemporary and new when they are advocated—then that is "bad" teaching, and perhaps even antiteaching? Of course, this is precisely not what we are saying. *Regardless of the content of belief,* "old" and "new," "old-fashioned" and "modern" do not determine the *being* of truth—and this fact is independent of *what* truth one may be referring to.

To illustrate again what antiteaching means: How many Catholic children in parochial schools have been taught that something is true *because* the Pope says so? It is only fair to say that this does not characterize Catholic-school teaching at its best, but also in all fairness one must admit that it has happened. Now, such teaching is perverse for two reasons. First, it is impossible for any proposition to *be* true *because* anyone says so. This holds for the Pope, as for anyone else. Second, it just so happens that if the child learns this, he is being "taught," under the guise of Catholicism, one of the worst of all heresies. The essence of Catholicism is that the Pope, when speaking *ex cathedra*, states a theological proposition *because* it is true; it is not true because he proclaims it. One may disagree with the truth-claim of the Pope when speaking *ex cathedra*. And a non-Catholic may honestly do so. But even an honest atheist knows that Catholicism is not to be rejected because the Pope "created truth." He rejects Catholicism, *not* because something is false *because* the Pope has proclaimed it true, but rather *because* the Pope "created truth." He rejects Catholicism, *not* because something is true—in the very meaning of the *being* of truth—that the Pope has proclaimed false.

The fact that both cannot be correct so far as the content of truth is concerned, is a matter, however interesting, that transcends our problem. It may be remarked, however—and this *is* interesting —that the nonideological atheist and the theist might both agree on the nature of teaching and learning—both being opposed only by their ideological counterparts.

KINDS OF KNOWLEDGE AND THEIR RELATIONS

The three orders, the order of being, the order of knowledge, and the order of teaching and learning, are related in certain ways. No one of them is reducible to another. The order of being refers to whatever exists or can exist; it is that about which one attempts to get knowledge. The pattern of order which is knowledge is itself a being, albeit of a nonmaterial kind, hence there can be knowledge about the nature of knowledge. There are concepts or categories distinctive of each order. An electron exists in the order of being. The "concept" of an electron does not so exist. A "concept" is a category in the order of knowledge, a logical instrument *by which* we know *what* real beings are. Hence, the order of knowledge must be founded upon the order of being.

A curricular category, such as a "course," is one in the order of teaching and learning. It, too, is an instrument, but one *by which* the teacher helps the student to learn some kind of knowledge. Hence, any curriculum must be founded upon the order of knowledge. The relation of the three orders to each other by way of presupposition, or "being founded upon," is not reversible. That is, the order of being as founded upon the order of knowledge, and that, in turn, as founded upon the order of teaching and learning, is impossible in any rational sense. But human beings are not always rational. The consequence of attempting to reverse the order is antiteaching, as well as educational antiintellectualism.

If the order of teaching and learning is founded upon, although not deducible from, the order of knowledge, then some understanding of the latter is necessary if order rather than disorder is to obtain in curricular matters and other teaching and learning activities. The *being* of truth has been identified. But there is also the problem of the modes of truth which define different kinds of knowledge. What different kinds of knowledge are there, and what relations do they have to each other by way of presupposition? In itself, this is a far too large a problem to be considered here, and it has been treated elsewhere.[1] Fortunately, it is not necessary. All that is needed is clarification of those principles which are relevant to the order of teaching and learning. By "relevant" we mean that the nature of the teaching-learning activity implies—i.e., presupposes—certain truths about the structure of knowledge. These principles will be made use of when we later investigate what a curriculum is.

There are innumerable names for what students "study," e.g., mathematics, physics, geology, typewriting, painting, automobile mechanics, ethics, history, humanities, social sciences, driver education, philosophy of history, government. It is immediately obvious that such a list, which could be increased by dozens of more names taken out of an educational catalogue, exhibits no order; it is just a list. To have any order, there must be some kind of classification.

---

[1] William Oliver Martin, *The Order and Integration of Knowledge*, Ann Arbor: University of Michigan Press, 1957.

There are two broad kinds of ordering: first, according to the structure which the things have that are being referred to, and second, for some human convenience.

A small plot of ground for a garden has a structure, in this case, square, quite independent of any unit of measurement. The sides may be measured in inches or centimeters, or any other units. The unit chosen may depend upon human convenience, but the nature of that which is measured is not, in its being, a function of human interest or convenience. It might have been rectangular instead of square, but if it is square then the length of a side is independent of the units chosen to measure it.

A biologist will classify "cat" in accordance with its essential nature, and its relations with other biological entities. However it is done, and it may not be easy, human conveniences and purposes are irrelevant—except, of course, for the very purpose itself. Yet, for human purposes it may be classified in many other ways, and by "it" reference is *not* to the word but to the object itself. One person sees the animal as a "pet," while another sees it as one among several kinds of "mice eliminators."

It can be said that the one kind of ordering is objective, the other is subjective. However, what is of importance is to recognize the relation between the two. Ordering according to human purposes is possible only because there is an objective order that *is* what it *is*, independent of such purposes. Neither kind of ordering is a substitute for the other. It is because the side of the square garden plot has a given length independent of the units chosen for measurement that such a choice is possible. It is because the cat has a nature and a history, individual and evolutionary, that it is possible to classify it in various ways according to human interests. To say it in another way, independent of human interests there can *be* no "pet," but the cat can *be* independent of such interests.

These two kinds of ordering can also be used in the ordering of knowledge, provided the same relation of presupposition of implication holds, and that neither one is reduced to the other. The one kind of ordering would seek to find how one kind of knowledge is ordered by way of evidence and truth to other kinds. If a student is to get to know biology in other than an elementary way, then a knowledge of chemistry is necessary. Now this proposition is *not* one on the level of the order of knowledge, but rather one on the level of the order of teaching and learning, for it is concerned with part of the curricular program for a student. If he is going very far in biology, then he must take one or more courses in chemistry. He may have the freedom to choose or not to choose to pursue biology that far. But, if he so chooses, then he is bound by an objective necessity which is quite independent of choice or interests.

What is the foundation of, the very reason for the being of, such a necessity, and which in this case is an objective order in the curricular order? The foundation lies in an objective order of knowledge, which is also not a matter of choice. The following proposition *is* on the level of the order of knowledge, and constitutes the ground for the truth of the proposition in the order of teaching and learning: Some propositions in chemistry are constitutive as evidence, in part, for the truth of some propositions in biology. Now the truth of this proposition has nothing whatsoever to do with choices, interests, or purposes—other than, of course, the choice, interest, or purpose of human beings seeking the truth, for in such seeking all other interests are subordinate.

Were it not for the human mind there could be no propositions, no truth to be known, no knowledge, and therefore no knowledge about the nature of knowledge. But the *being* of the truth is determined by the other end of the bi-polar relation. Hence, the truth of the proposition above must have its *being* in an objective order, in this case the order of knowledge, which order is to be discovered. This means that each kind of knowledge must have an essential nature which makes it what it is, just that kind of knowledge and not some other kind. Were it not so, one could not even talk about a kind of knowledge, for there would be no referent.

To discover the order of knowledge has not been an easy task. Man's knowledge has a history, a development. Different kinds of knowledge had to emerge, they were not given already made and formed in man's early history. What later became kinds of knowledge were at one time blurred together. In the ancient Greek and Egyptian civilizations, there was the emergence of mathematics and physics—of a sort, for the term "physics" had a much broader meaning for Aristotle than it has today for the theoretical physicist.

To Pythagoras, it was clear that mathematics had to do with numbers, but he did not, and could not, know the difference between quantity, number, metric, and magnitude. Is mathematics limited to numbers? Or is number a kind of quantity, and has mathematics as its formal object, quantity? Metaphysics and logic, in any systematic sense, came into being with Plato and Aristotle. The experimental sciences, in the sense that we know them today, emerge in medieval and modern times.

With the development of kinds of knowledge came certain serious problems—not merely problems internal to a kind of knowledge, but problems having to do with the relation between kinds of knowledge. What are the separate domains of mathematics, astronomy, and theology? Where does the one begin and end, for any kind of knowledge is of necessity limited to this and not that? The *nature* of anything also defines its limits. And so with knowledge. Was Galileo unclear as to the demarkations of the subjects just mentioned? Were certain theologians unclear as to the limitations of theology? Did Kepler confuse mathematics and metaphysics? An affirmative answer would be demanded by the fruits of scholarship.

This does not at all mean that because, in any given historical era, the limits of a kind of knowledge were unclear and difficult to define, that therefore there are not different kinds of knowledge. Nor does it mean that there is only one kind, or that one kind can be a substitute for another. There can be such difficulties only because there are kinds of knowledge, the structured relations of which need to be understood. Again, one kind of knowledge cannot be a substitute for another, for otherwise it wouldn't be *that* kind as distinct from another. The biologist has difficulty in determining where plants end and animals begin, but it would be foolish to infer from this that there are no plants or animals. The converse is the case, for it is only because they exist that he has the problem. Nor is anything solved by reducing all knowledge to one kind, say, "science." In this case, the result would not be science, but "scient*ism*." And, strictly speaking, this would better be called ideology rather than philosophy. It would be equally ideological to reduce all knowledge to "theology," in which case we would have, not theology any longer but rather "theolog*ism*."

But all of this is "war," or would be if continued. However, kinds of knowledge are innocent in themselves. For example, the so-called "warfare between science and theology" is a misstatement of fact because of a misunderstanding of the *locus* of the struggle. The conflict was not between science and theology, but rather between some (not all) scient*ists* and some (not all) theolog*ians*, all of whom were, to some extent, unclear about the limitations of their own fields.

The necessity for clarification of the order of knowledge has become all the more urgent in recent times because of the rise of mass education and the multiplication of curricular categories representing departments and schools and colleges. This has given rise to a tendency toward institutional determination of the nature of knowledge. This is the very reverse of the correct procedure, which rationally demands that curricular programs and institutional entities be founded upon—the minimal meaning being "not incompatible with"—the order of knowledge which, as has been pointed out, is what it is independent of institutional purposes, especially of the prestige of "departments" or "faculties."

With all of this in mind, let us now return to the list of "studies" which students can make when they are in our contemporary schools. Questions can be asked. Given the list of "names," to what do they refer? Is there any order in the listing? Do the names represent several different kinds of classification? To study the one, what do you have to know about the others? Do these names stand for kinds of knowledge, courses (which are curricular artifacts) *in* a kind of knowledge; and, if so, then a theoretical kind of knowledge or a practical sort? Does one name refer to a group-category which really means "miscellaneous" (which also means that no one knows exactly what to do with the items), and another name to a group-category referring to several kinds of knowledge, all using the same method? Or, are they merely "names" which can be ordered any way one wishes, say, in alphabetical order? Of course, for human convenience they can be ordered alphabetically in the back of a catalogue.

As we have mentioned before, careful studies have been made in answer to these questions. It will be sufficient for our purpose to give a brief account in order that we may finally show their relevance to teaching and learning activities.

EXISTENTIAL AND FORMAL OBJECTS

For our purpose, and without becoming too technical, it will be sufficient to think of what is called the "formal object" as the aspect of existence studied. Living things in nature may be studied from the standpoint of physics, chemistry, and biology. Different aspects of the same existential objects are abstracted and analysed, thus giving rise to the different science categories. From that which is nonliving, e.g., a grain of sand, nothing can be abstracted (*drawn from* it) that could give rise to a biological aspect. Once a certain aspect is defined, then it may be studied in and of itself, and is applicable to anything in the world having the said characteristics. Physics and chemistry are applicable, as sciences, to anything in the world that is material, including human beings. Biology and all of its subdivisions deal with living matter.

The sciences mentioned are "theoretical," for they are concerned primarily not with practice, not with "knowing how," but with the pure knowing of an aspect of existence. They are also "positive" sciences in so far as they abstract from the ontological, i.e., the metaphysical and the theological.

One name found on a list of "studies" is geology. Is it a science such as the others mentioned? A science, yes, but not like the others, for geology is not defined by a formal object, but rather by the existential object studied, namely, the earth's crust. The geologist makes use of the physical sciences when he gets knowledge about this existential object. Hence, it would be an error in ordering to put geology on the same coordinate level of classification as physics, chemistry, and biology. Like astronomy, it has an "historical" nature.

This error is, however, often reflected in the college curriculum. A student may be allowed to choose among the "sciences." It seems that it doesn't make much difference what he "takes" to be "liberally" educated, as long as he gets "some science." So the geology professor may end up with a lot of students who know no physics, chemistry, or biology, or at least not enough of each subject to be useful. In some cases, the students may even choose geology in order to escape these other "hard core" sciences. (In one university in the United States, a course in astronomy was introduced into the curriculum of "general" education and advertised as requiring "no knowledge of mathematics," and it was amazing the number of students who became interested!)

THEORETICAL KNOWLEDGE

Theoretical kinds of knowledge are those which have a structure independent of any use-value to which they may be put. They are concerned with existence, with aspects of being, with modes of being, with "the way things are." Each of these phrases is in itself inexact. Further clarification will come when the practical subjects are contrasted with the theoretical. There is (1) the "knowing of being," (2) the "knowing how to do," and (3) the "knowing how to make." The latter two define the "practical" kinds of knowledge.

Examples of theoretical knowledge are physics, chemistry, biology, botany, mathematics, ethics (as distinct from morals), esthetics, the philosophy of history, metaphysics. And yet these are not all theoretical in the same way. Some are theoretical and autonomous, and others are theoretical and synthetic.

Physics and metaphysics would be examples of autonomy. This means that no other kind of knowledge enters into them constitutively as evidence. Mathematics is necessary for physics, but is related to physics only instrumentally, i.e., no truth in mathematics proves or demonstrates physical order, although physical order will exemplify mathematical patterns. Metaphysics is concerned with that kind of abstraction by which one arrives at the most universal of all categories—essence, existence, being, actuality and potentiality, substance, quantity, quality, etc. Through abstraction from experience, and reflective analysis, propositions are formed the truth of which do not require other kinds of knowledge as evidence. That any finite thing does not exist necessarily, but only contingently, is an example of a metaphysical proposition, whether or not it be true or false. The dialectical materialism of Marxism contains certain fundamental metaphysical principles stating the relation between quantity and quality, although, for certain historical reasons, Marxists prefer the term "ontological" rather than "metaphysical."

The philosophy of history is theoretical, but synthetic and not autonomous, for it is a synthesis of history (as positive) and the ontological, i.e., the metaphysical and/or theological. The evidence from two kinds of knowledge is necessary in order to know the truth of any proposition of the philosophy of history. That Moses liberated a host of people by leading them out of Egypt in the 13th century B.C., is a purely historical proposition. And so is its denial. But that Moses did this as a divine mission given him by God, that is a proposition of the philosophy of history. And so would be the proposition denying it. The first proposition may be relatively substantiated or not by the ordinary methods of historiography which the historian uses. No ontological evidence is required. However, such evidence is required for the second proposition.

If there is no ontological knowledge, i.e., no metaphysical and/or theological knowledge, then there can be no philosophy of history. Man is limited to the knowledge that this or that happened, limited to history in its "positive" sense. Since there is reason to believe that man is not, never was, and cannot be, satisfied with such negativism and skepticism, the only alternative to the ontological is the ideological; in which case man *imposes* meanings upon history, the meanings varying according to the different use-purposes to which they are put.

The implications of all this for the curriculum of liberal education are many. How can a student be required to take history but not philosophy? Is he not to learn anything of the meaning of history? If he does, how does he learn it? Not by reading his own meanings into history. From his teacher of history? If so, where did the teacher get his knowledge? In the same way the student is getting his? And so on.

The philosophy of history is an example of knowledge, if knowledge it is, that is theoretical and synthetic with respect to "being." But there is also synthetic, theoretical knowledge with respect to "doing" and "making." Human conduct is "doing," and ethics is the theoretical knowledge concerned with the principles in terms of which human doing is judged as good or bad, right or wrong. Ethics is to be distinguished from law, medicine, political science, and the social sciences, which are all practical, for they are concerned with "knowing how to do." Attention is to be called to the fact that because of the constant confusion between knowledge and curricular categories, especially when labeled with the same words, the distinction made is likely to be misunderstood. With this in mind, we may recall that the order of teaching and learning, hence a curricular category such as a "course," should be compatible with whatever is true about the nature of knowledge. Courses and departmental "subjects" of study are to be appraised in terms of the distinction, and not conversely.

The distinction made may be illustrated by considering the difference between law and ethics. What justice is, is a problem in ethics, and as such is theoretical. The principles that constitute justice as a virtue are determined, so far as their truth is concerned, by an appeal to the nature of man in relation to his origin and destiny, and which of necessity brings in the ontological. Now, given such ethical knowledge, there is the further problem of *knowing how* to act in concrete circumstances so as to put the principles into *practice*. The discipline called "law," i.e., the positive law which is humanly created, not discovered, is one way of doing this. As with any other practical subject, law does not furnish its own principles. When the law is studied in relation to the ethical principles upon which law must rest—if there is to be justice and not tyranny—then the subject studied is called "jurisprudence."

The proposition to the effect that it is far worse to commit injustice than to suffer it, is a proposition of ethics, and one at least as old as Plato. It is theoretical, and the evidence as to its truth or falsity rests upon the *being* of man and the *being* of the reality into which and through which he is born and dies. It is not the kind of knowledge that is "knowing how to do." Rather, it is the kind of knowledge, if the proposition is true, in terms of which practical knowledge, the "knowing how to do," can be partially acquired.

To illustrate, if the proposition is true, then the intelligent Negro of goodwill will realize that, although it is not good to suffer injustice from the white man, nevertheless the evil must be corrected through the law, at least in part. But, in so changing matters by the law, one must *know how* to do it without creating the inverse situation in which the Negro now does injustice to white people. Why? Because it is far worse to commit injustice than to suffer it. The law is concerned with the "knowing how" in this case, but the law presupposes the theoretical ethical principle which explains "why."

It is most important to emphasize that the principle of the order of knowledge which has been illustrated is not dependent upon the truth or falsity of the proposition used in the illustration. Even a false proposition in ethics is still a proposition *of* ethics, and not of some other subject. A proposition of any kind of knowledge is defined in terms of its formal object, not its truth. In fact, with regard to the truth or falsity of any proposition, one must know what kind of proposition it is, to what kind of knowledge it belongs, before one can know what kind of evidence is or is not relevant to its truth or falsity. If I am talking about the cardinal number system and say that two plus two equals fifty-six, then, even though the proposition is false, I am still "talking" mathematics and not any other kind of knowledge. I have simply uttered a false proposition in mathematics—but it is mathematics and not physics or history.

With this in mind, let us reconsider the original ethical proposition, and let us suppose that someone denies it. He does not escape formulating an ethical proposition. He merely has another one—one which is, if we may beg the question for the moment, probably false. Yet, it is still a proposition *of* ethics—and not a proposition of physics, mathematics, etc. And so, let us say that it is much better to inflict injustice than to suffer it, for that is the difference between being smart and being a sucker. Now, acting upon this principle the Negro will try, through the power of numbers and by means of the law or otherwise, to inflict injustice upon the white people just as they have inflicted it upon the Negroes. One can say that this is a false "ethic," or that it is "ethical nihilism," but one can only say this because the proposition involved is on the level of the "ethical," i.e., it is not a false proposition *of* any other kind of knowledge. Whether one attempts to uphold or to refute the proposition, he is dealing with an ethical problem. Even if one wishes to call such a statement nonsensical, it is still "ethical nonsense," and not some other kind.

Esthetics is the philosophical discipline which has to do with the theoretical aspect of "how to make," primarily in the fine arts, and secondarily in the use arts. Music, poetry, painting, sculpture, architecture, and literature are humanly created artifacts. However much the various art mediums may differ, they are all works of art because they have something in common, namely, esthetic value, whether conceived of in terms of beauty or in some other manner. In studying any given fine art, the student is learning how something is *made*. In studying esthetics, he is concerned with those principles of esthetic value in terms of which what is made can be appraised.

Esthetics, like ethics, is synthetic as well as theoretical, for it looks two ways. Ethical principles cannot be merely deduced from the ontological. They must also take into account the various kinds of evidence from the sciences of man. And so, esthetic principles must take into account what and how man "makes" as well as the ontological. On the other hand, were it not for the ontological considerations, esthetics would vanish, for it would be reduced to the purely subjective.

PRACTICAL KNOWLEDGE

Practical knowledge is defined as that knowledge which is concerned with "knowing how to do" and "knowing how to make," and not primarily with knowing kinds or modes of *being*.

Knowledge of "how to do" is concerned with human conduct. There are two fundamental kinds of doing—doing with respect to other persons, and doing with respect to things. The first defines the moral sciences, which are also called "social sciences." Examples of these would be economics, government, political science, law, medicine. Tree surgery and veterinary medicine are concerned with knowing how to do something with respect to things.

Practical and theoretical knowledge are distinct, but not separable, for the theoretical explains the "why" of the "know-how." This is the case even for the simplest of acts. One may learn how to move a large rock with a crowbar; the principle of the lever explains why you do it this way and not that way.

The moral sciences are practical because they are concerned with *how to act*, how to conduct oneself with respect to other persons. Hence, they have to do with *means* primarily, and only secondarily with ethical principles by way of presupposition. Herein lies the distinction between the "moral" and the "ethical," two terms often used as synonyms—and they may so be used where the distinction is not relevant. To be accurate, however, one should speak of "ethical principles" and "moral means," the latter *by way of action* relating principles to a concrete set of circumstances, the situation. If there were no circumstances, there could be no moral problem. If there were no ethical principles, alternative means could not be appraised; instrumental action by way of means would still remain, but it could not be called "moral" or "immoral."

These distinctions may not seem very important, and their relevance to teaching and learning may not be clear. In fact, however, the contrary is the case. If curricular programing does not recognize them, serious miseducation or "antieducation" can be the consequence.

There are those who do not like the term "ethical principles." It has an "absolutist" ring about it. Why not speak rather of "ends" in relation to "means," in which case morality consists in the continuity of the means-ends relation, each being adjusted to the other accordingly as there is an experimental testing of the consequences? This will be recognized as the position of "Instrumentalism," associated with the pragmatism of John Dewey and his followers. Now a full critique of this position has been done many times, and there is neither time nor place here for a repetition. Keeping in mind that Dewey was not always consistent, and that he was not at all happy with many of his followers, let us proceed to point out three serious confusions in instrumentalism and their effect on teaching and learning.

The first thing to be cleared up is the difference between the philosophical and the ideological use of the term "absolute." The terms "absolute" and "relative" are correlative, like the terms "east and west," "husband and wife." The one can have meaning only if the other has meaning. Earlier, we had occasion to point out that there can be no "east" if there is no "west." One cannot say, intelligently, that "everything is east." Similarly, one cannot say that everything is relative and there are no absolutes. Nor can one say that everything is absolute and nothing is relative. If they are said, they are uttered as ideological slogans. Usually the person is not aware of the philosophical implications, and often doesn't care. But he does have a vague idea, sufficient for him, of the *use* of the slogan. As a weapon it eliminates that which would prevent him from creating his "own ethics." (This may also take a social as well as an individualistic form.) Philosophically speaking, the person has switched absolutes. But, if he is ill-prepared, because of ignorance, ill will, or both, either to understand or justify his *own* absolute, then he may mask it all with an ideological slogan. This forces the person who disagrees, if unsophisticated in such matters, to "argue" equally ideologically. This, of course, is a recipe for fruitlessness, and the end result is despair and cynicism in matters philosophical.

The philosophical problem is: What is the correct *locus* of that which is absolute? With respect to the problem at hand, if there is something in terms of which all human interests, individual and/or collective, can be measured and appraised, then such interests are relative to *it*. If not, then human interests in one form or another become absolute, and everything else is relative. The real issue is *what* is absolute and *what* is relative. The assertion that there are true ethical principles means, at the minimum, that changing and variable human interests are not the ultimate court of appeal, but must themselves stand under judgment. It is this that enabled the Hebrew people, thousands of years ago, to transcend the mythology of the tribal god. It is this which enables those fighting for justice for the Negro to give a reason *why* for their concern and commitment—for one cannot rationally make an appeal merely in terms of the caprice of subjective preference. The denial, literally, that there are true ethical principles is to reduce the ethical to nothing at all; hence, the term "ethical nihilism." It is perhaps safe to say that most of those who make utterances implying such nihilism really do not mean it. Unfortunately, some do.

A note should be made of further confusion attending the term "moral," if the possibility of ethical knowledge is denied. A person may say: "We do not deny morality at all. All societies, at different times and in different places, have moral standards. But of course they differ, and who is to say which is correct?" Now it is well known that when a concept is abandoned, the *word* may remain and be used for quite a different reference. Here is a case in point. What is being said is that all societies have "a way of life," they make value judgments, etc. Now this is a tautological truism, banal as well as irrelevant. The word "moral" refers to a fact, the way *in fact* people live, whether or not they ought to live that way, and independent of the question of good or bad, right or wrong. The final ambiguity is in the "who is to say . . ." The question is rhetorical and cannot be taken seriously. For the person who asks is usually not the one who cares. The difficulty may arise because there are or are not any ethical principles. If the first, then let us reasonably and cooperatively seek the answer. If the second, then no one can "say," hence the question is irrelevant.

The second confusion is this. It is sometimes said: there are no so-called ethical principles independent of consequences; rather the consequences themselves should be the "judge." Let there be alternative *means* of action X, Y, and Z. Find the consequences of each possible alternative, and choose according to these consequences. If X, then a, b. If Y, then c, d, and if Z, then e, f. Now, how do we choose? There are three sets of consequences, but they, of themselves, do not alone inform one which is best. Choose the alternative that has the most desirable set, namely, X. But in this case, desires and interests are the standard, and not the consequences at all. The consequences, a, b, are chosen because they *conform* best to certain interests. But this is not enough, for the moral problem is what interests are or are not to be pursued ethically. Left on the level of the "instrumental" alone, we have the formalistic fallacy in ethics. The Nazi gauleiter Eichmann, was evidently extremely rational, instrumentally. "If we burn the Jews, then time will be saved, and it will cost less; if we bury the Jews, then we must acquire land, the money to buy it, etc.; if we put the Jews in prison, then. . . ." As history tells us, the first alternative was chosen.

Now, if there is no ethical knowledge, it is not fair to protest, for that would be merely expressing a subjective preference, an emotion, or something of that sort. It is not sufficient to say or to imply that "One really can't say whether such action is right or wrong, but Oh! Horrors! I wouldn't want to do such a thing, and I would prefer that the Nazis not do it, too." In terms of ethical principles, i.e., rationally, such killing of the Jews was wrong. The appeal has to be made in terms of the ethical principles of justice, natural rights, etc.

Nor will it help to say that in our example we have not considered all the alternatives, and that we have selected out a "bad" set. Formally and instrumentally, the Nazis could have been aware of *every* alternative. The point remains that the consequences were not the judge, but rather their interests, and the consequences were chosen because they best *conformed* to their interests.

There have been several suggestions on how to avoid all this and yet not admit ethical knowledge. It has been said that what the Nazis did was bad because the consequences were antisocial. Now, this is no answer at all, for the question is begged. If there are true ethical principles, then such action was antisocial only in the sense that it is anti-the-society-I-would-prefer.

Another tack that has been taken is: Choose according to consequences in the long run, not the immediate consequences. Such a procedure is necessary, but not sufficient, for one is faced with an infinite, or at least indefinite, series of consequences such that, "no matter how far one goes" one is right where one started. For as we have pointed out, the consequences themselves have to be appraised.

An idealistic version of this takes the turn that, yes, there is the absolute as well as the relative; but the ethical absolute-good or standard is an ideal to which an asymptotic approach is made through a continuous series of means-ends reactions. However, there is an ambiguity lurking here. If the so-called "ideal" is simply a human creation as an expression of interests, then, once again, we are back to where we started, plus, in this case, a pious hope. On the other hand, if the "ideal" is realistically grounded, is a norm, has content, and can be *known* and not merely *held*, then we have ethical knowledge—which means that instrumenta*lism* is

Knowledge as the Formal Cause in Teaching and Learning 131

not sufficient, for there is normative as well as instrumental truth.

The analysis thus far has not been concerned with the question of *what* ethical principles are true. That is an ethical problem, whereas our problem has been concerned with the moral and ethical as knowledge, and specifically, *what* is presupposed or implied if there is to be knowledge on the level of "moral means."

The third confusion that tends to break down the distinction between ethical principles and moral means has to do with the notion of the continuity of means and ends. This notion has already been analyzed to some degree. Specifically, however, we refer to the tendency to use the term "end" in two quite different ways —at one time meaning an ethical principle, and at another time referring to a remote means in a series of means-ends relations. Often the ambiguity is not serious, for in a given context the distinction may not be relevant. Again, often the context itself clarifies. The ambiguity is a serious one if it leads to elimination of the distinction completely. We may illustrate by considering an example.

A group of Negroes is marching towards the Capital of the state of Alabama. One of them is asked why he is doing this, and he answers in terms of justice, natural rights, and human dignity. Now these are ends in the sense of ethical principles. There are "principles" involved, he says, and he is willing to struggle for them. Justice is a cardinal virtue; it is not a means on the level of action, not even a remote means that can be called an end. Rather, "justice" refers to certain principles in terms of which all action in terms of the means-ends series is to be judged, no matter how remote the latter means (meaning end) may be.

Another Negro is asked why he is marching, and he replies (A) that he and others want to see the governor. Why? Because (B) we want to have the right to register and vote. Why? So that (C) by voting we can eliminate other discriminating practices. Here is a continuity of means-ends relations, not on the level of ethical principle, but on the level of action; and all moral means are on that level. In this case, the term "end" refers to one means in relation to others. Following the example, A is a means to B, and B is a means to C. But, depending upon its relation, B is both a means and an end. In relation to A, B is an end. In relation to C,

B is a means. When the term "end" is used in this way it really refers to one means among others in a series of means. When the term is used in the first sense it refers to an ethical principle in terms of which the whole series is to be appraised. The continuity of means-ends, therefore, so far from implicitly denying the being of ethical knowledge, really presupposes it—that is, if we are to talk of moral means, and not of mere technique.

It may be pointed out that the means-ends relation still is sufficient, and that our analysis is really essentially on a verbal level. For, on what we call "principles," is there not the same relation of means to ends? Why are you marching? I want my natural rights (principle). Why? Because I insist on human dignity (principle). Why? Because I want to be happy (principle, i.e., happiness as a principle). Why? Because God created me as a human being, destined for Heaven, and to which this life is. . . . Do we not have a series of means-ends relations on what we call principles?

No, not at all, except verbally. The reason that it seems to be so is that, just as the term "end" is used ambiguously, so is the term "means." In this example, the term "means" is used to refer to a hierarchy of principles, one being subordinate to another. Earthly dignity and happiness is a *principle*, in terms of which a *program of action* (moral means) is constructed. But even so, earthly happiness is subordinate to a higher principle which always takes precedence—in fact, gives the rationale to the subordinate principle—namely, God's Love and Will for man's ultimate happiness in Heaven.

The distinctions can be pinpointed and also summed up this way. Moral codes (such as, say, a "better business" code), positive law, governmental policies, economic programs, health programs are all on the level of action, doing; they are on the level of moral means, the *knowing how* to do just acts, etc. And every moral means is a human creation when the plan of action is considered in abstraction from the action itself. However, the knowing which is on the level of ethical principle (e.g., all the virtues, such as courage, justice, honesty, etc.) is not a *knowing how*, it is *knowing of being*. As such, ethical principles are *discovered*, not created. *It is ideologies which are created and not discovered.* Human actions are appraised in terms of ethical principles, but the principles themselves are not actions, not doings.

The order of knowledge should help to explain, and not be determined by, the vagaries of language. The journalist will speak of "the new, emerging ethic," especially with regard to matters of sex. Here "ethic" refers usually, not to ethical principles, but to a new moral code, a readaptation of means in the light of changing circumstances. Moral means are of necessity "relative" in the sense that they have no truth-meaning or being except in so far as they *relate* ethical principles to changing personal and social situations. However, it would be relativ*ism* in the subjective sense (which is ethical nihilism) to say that the truth of ethical principles is merely a function of the changing environment. If Plato's statement, that it is far worse to commit injustice than to suffer it, is true, then it is always true; for it is based upon the being and nature of human beings. What varies down through the ages is the ways in which one can both inflict and suffer injustice.

Of course, one can deny that there is any ethical knowledge at all, and then consistently work out the implications for education. A few have done so. Ideology takes over, and philosophy vanishes (though the name may remain). "Use-value" becomes a substitute for truth. Such consistency is usually sufficient to cause one to "go down in history." But most people who seem to deny ethical knowledge do not really do so. In their inconsistency they flounder morally; since they attempt to do that which rationally can not be done. For example, a person may deny the "natural-law" ethic on Saturday night if it is believed it will interfere with his "sex freedom"; but he may vehemently invoke it the next day on the Sunday march in defense of the Negro who is discriminated against by the "positive law."

The moral sciences, e.g., political science, law, medicine, etc., are moral to the degree that they look both to concrete existential conditions *and* ethical principles. And to that degree, they are "social" too. Otherwise, they are reduced to ideological instruments of tyranny.

On the educational level, and especially in liberal education, what is true in the order of knowledge must be reflected in the curricular program. A teacher of "social subjects" must have some knowledge, and the more the better, of ethics, systematic and historical, in order to teach and not merely "condition" or "determine attitudes" of students. In any case, the teacher will have opinions and the students will have attitudes. The relevant issue for the order of teaching and learning is this: Does the teacher have his opinions because he has ethical knowledge or because he lacks it; and are the students' opinions "determined" because they have acquired such knowledge or because they haven't?

THE FINE ARTS

Practical knowledge is found in the moral, religious, and artistic disciplines. The first two disciplines are concerned with how to do, the third with how to make something. Before proceeding further, let us keep in mind that the problem we are dealing with is not an ethical or an esthetic one. Rather, it is the kind of knowledge which the moral and the ethical is; and similarly for the arts. Knowing about acting is knowing and not acting; and knowing about making is knowing and not making.

Music, poetry, painting, sculpture, and literature are examples of the "fine arts"; technology, agriculture, and engineering in all their forms are examples of the "use arts." In all of these art activities concerned with making, there is also a sizeable amount of doing. What is the difference? There are only two "things" one can perfect, a "fact" or an "artifact." By a "fact" we refer to a nature given, and by "artifact" to a nature made. The former is relevant to doing and acting. There is an art to medical practice, but medicine is a moral science, for it has to do with perfecting human beings with respect to health. The bodily nature of a human being is given not made, and the aim is to perfect that nature. The same is true for veterinary medicine. The aim is not to make a dog, but to help a given dog get well. In acting or doing, the good of that which is acted upon is ultimate, whereas, in making something, that which is acted upon is purely instrumental to the perfection of the artifact, that which is to be made.

What is distinct may not be separable. Doing is instrumental to knowing, and conversely. And so there may be a great amount of doing in the process of making. In the construction of a bridge, for example, various kinds of moral and social actions are necessary. Likewise, making may be instrumental to doing, e.g., a building may be constructed in order that judges and the courts may do their work. Although not separable, making and doing are distinct; otherwise, they could not each be instrumental to the other as practical activities.

Through the ambiguity of words, the distinction may appear to break down. In doing and acting with respect to other people, do we not "make" or "remake" them? Does not the teacher, in a sense, make or remake the nature of the student? Yes, but the "sense" is a way of speaking. A child is a potential man, independent of anyone's purpose. Hence, the purpose of the teacher *qua* teacher is to help perfect the nature of the child, and one way of helping him is through teaching. On the other hand, to the artist, the maker, what is a piece of clay potentially? It could be most anything—a brick for a house or raw material for a vase. What it *becomes* depends on the purpose of the artist. The artist *uses* the clay; his aim is not to perfect it. In perfecting human nature, the end is given; in perfecting a work of art, the end is humanly determined. If the distinction is broken down, then the implications are serious for the classroom. For the very being and nature of the student now becomes merely raw material instrumental to the purpose of the teacher. In which case, again, we have antiteaching rather than teaching.

The distinction between the fine arts and the use arts is not an arbitrary one, nor merely a "class" distinction as some have thought. In the use arts, there is a distinction between the maker and the user, although the two may be the same. In the fine arts, there is the distinction between the maker and the experiencer, although, again, the two may be the same. In the fine arts, there is esthetic value, concerned with beauty in its various modes. Hence, there are two kinds of "knowing how"—knowing how to make, and knowing how to appreciate what is made. Esthetic value is peculiarly related to feeling in a way in which moral values are not. To put it simply, from the standpoint of the fine arts, feelings are, in part, the judge; the "appraiser," so to speak. However, "blind" feeling can hardly be a judge. Hence, there is the problem of knowing how to *appreciate* a work of fine art, as well as knowing how to make it. Esthetics is the philosophical discipline concerned with the theoretical principles of esthetic value. As theoretical, esthetics is knowing, and not knowing how.

These distinctions on the level of the order of knowledge have implications for the order of teaching and learning. Not everyone can be an artist in the sense of knowing how to make. Nevertheless, somewhere along the way, the student should have some acquaintance with this kind of knowledge. What is of more importance is the education of the student in *appreciation*. This will require introducing him, especially on the level of liberal education, to the study of esthetics. The point to be made is that in experiencing a work of fine art, a person will respond emotionally. But there is a great deal of difference between whether he responds in a certain way because he has esthetic knowledge or because he lacks it. This kind of knowledge enters, constitutively, into appreciation, which is a kind of contemplation, and also into "art criticism." In terms of esthetic principles, the student will learn how to be critical, how to appraise intelligently, and also how to increase his appreciation in the art forms. Both animals and humans "feel." However, animals do not create poetry or buildings, and then become critical of them after attempting to appreciate them. That is the difference between parrots and beavers on the one hand, and human beings on the other. In man, the relation between feeling and intellect is such that *what is felt depends partly upon what man knows*.

It is important to understand—and the good art teacher should have such understanding—the converse instrumentality between knowing and feeling. Through feeling one may get to know something, and through knowing one may get to feel in a certain way. It must be emphasized that in the fine arts one does not make something in order to know it. Rather, the purpose is that of esthetic feeling, feeling of a certain quality. In studying esthetics, the purpose is to know in order to make; and secondly, in order to obtain a response of a certain quality, to experience properly that which is made.

In teaching, the teacher of esthetics will have to know something about the arts, and the art teacher will have to have some knowledge of esthetics. Only too often this is not the case in the school, which makes questionable what goes on under the name of "art" in the curriculum. The student should have both kinds of knowledge, but he is not likely to get it if his teacher does not have it. This does not mean that the student in the early grades must be taught esthetics in a systematic manner. Remembering that from the standpoint of pedagogy the psychological may take priority over the logical, it is obvious that the stress in the early years of education may well be on the making, and certainly not on "art criticism." However, as the student moves up the educational ladder, there comes a time when he should learn the "why" of his making, and to do this he must study esthetics. Otherwise, he merely continues to "make"—which may have "fun" value, and, in the case of frustrated housewives, even "therapeutic" value. However, it is a corruption of art to reduce it either to fun or to therapy, although there will always be plenty of people to reap the economic rewards of such corruption. It is an understatement to say that such practice should not dignify the classroom. Art may be used for therapeutic purposes. Yes. But art *is not* therapy. There is a difference between what fine art *is* and what it may be *used* for. If this distinction is not made, then an art nihilism, or an esthetic nihilism, eventuates; just as, we may recall, there is such a thing as moral nihilism or ethical nihilism. Let us turn to this, and in doing so give a nonarbitrary definition of such nihilism; for, if it were arbitrary, it would be worthless.

It is well known that one of the fallacies to which men are prone is the "illicit conversion of an 'A' proposition." Except in the case of a real definition, it does not follow that from "All A is B," that "therefore all B is A." From the fact that all forms of fascism have been supported by businessmen, it does not follow that all businessmen are fascists. Now, it so happens that, although it is true that all art is human making, it does not at all follow that all making is art. It is very easy to assume otherwise. Something that is not an artifact, e.g., a sunset or a sea shell, may have esthetic value, and something that is man-made may have none at all. The drawings on the wall of a public toilet are man-made, but it does not necessarily follow that they are works of fine art. The shape of the rectangular salt cake put out into the field for cows will alter as it is continually licked. The altered shape may be interesting, but it is not a work of sculpture—contrary to the opinion of an "art critic" who raved over such an object that one wit presented in an art show.

Art nihilism or esthetic nihilism means that there is the denial of esthetic knowledge, just as moral or ethical nihilism means that there is no ethical knowledge. Esthetics is a theoretical, not a practical, discipline. Fine art is practical, but only on its own level of means. The immediate purpose for which a work of fine art is made is not a practical one. Rather, the purpose is an end in itself, with an esthetic value of some kind, even though a more remote end may be some use value. But in this case it has use value only because it first has esthetic value.

Knowing how to make a beautiful artifact does not necessarily imply knowledge as to *why* it is beautiful. And conversely. Although distinct, the two kinds of knowledge should not be separated, and the proper type of education will not separate them. Hence, esthetic knowledge will be introduced to the student gradually through his educational career, and on the level of liberal education he will study esthetics systematically. This is a curricular demand, and not something to be left to the whim of the student to elect or not to elect. Such necessity is not based upon the autocratic will of the makers of curricula, but rather is rooted in human nature itself. Whatever else he may be, the human being is a feeling creature. He cannot elect in life to feel or not to feel. The alternatives are whether he will feel with or without the knowledge he can have because he has an intellect, whether or not he knows why he enjoys this and not that, and whether or not his feelings are grounded in something that transcends them as a normative guide. If esthetics is absent on the curricular level, then it implies either a neglect or a denial of the possibility of esthetics as one kind of knowledge among others.

With some people, this conclusion will not be popular, and to others it will seem just plainly false. The protest may be as follows. A rational case can be made for the necessity of "art education." Certainly the student should be introduced to one or more of the arts in a relatively rigorous manner and to the extent that time will allow. But that esthetics, a philosophical discipline, is equally necessary is a *non sequitur*. It is certainly not necessary in order to "learn how to make." The great works of art were created by artists who knew little if anything about esthetics. Perhaps most of them did not even know the meaning of the word, assuming they ever heard of it. Did Shakespeare, Da Vinci, or Bach study esthetics? Or did the makers of the Parthenon? Esthetics may be desirable in the liberal education curriculum, but certainly it is not necessary.

In answering, we may admit that the facts mentioned are true. What is questionable is their relevance. The purpose of studying esthetics is not a professional one, to make everyone artists, but rather to aid one in understanding and appreciating what the professionals have done—even though in making their artifacts they may or may not have had conscious esthetic knowledge. In fact, the critic "proves" too much. People thought correctly long before the first logician. Had it not been so, there would not have been anything to reflect on in order to develop that knowledge which is logic. Likewise, there were good and bad actions performed by people long before there developed the kind of knowledge which is ethics. And we may be sure that Jesus never studied theology, although he did read the ancient religious writings, which is something quite different. But these are hardly reasons for eliminating logic, ethics, and theology from liberal education. If one wishes to do so, he must find better reasons.

A theoretical kind of knowledge should not be made to serve impossible purposes; and neither should a practical kind of knowledge. A physicist may not be able to repair his automobile engine, and the auto mechanic may know little, if any, physics. A saint may not know theology, and a theologian may not be very saintly. And a professor of ethics may not *know how* to live well with other people. There are analogies in other fields. For example, there are some who know little if any calculus, but who *know how* to "solve" a differential equation by graphing.

The moral of all this is that an educational norm is hardly to be determined by what *can* take place, or by what *has* happened. It is perhaps relevant, even though one runs the risk of an *ad hominem* argument or perhaps of begging the question, to point out that the subjectivism as regards values in recent times has made people increasingly insensitive to even the need for the theoretical in art. It is precisely *because* art has a peculiar relation to feeling that other kinds of knowledge do not have, that it is most subject to the corruption of subjectivism. For example, it is difficult to be a "phony" in physics or mathematics. But, unfortunately, it is not so in art. Even though a person may do minimal thinking, unfortunately he may do maximal feeling. In fact, the "phony" is almost defined by this relation. There is no quicker way of getting "cultured" than getting "interested" in art.

One kind of knowledge is not a substitute for another kind, either for education or for any other purpose. Esthetics is limited by its nature and purpose, as is any other kind of knowledge. But, if one is to escape from a routine, pedestrian kind of education in the arts, if one is to be liberated from shallowness, then he will need to study esthetics. The various arts give "range" in art education. It is esthetics that will give "depth," and also in the process enable one to understand the unity of the arts; for any given art is that which is to be seen in the light of the whole, since it cannot provide the wholeness itself.

Either there is or there is not esthetic knowledge. If there is no knowledge, then fine art tends to be reduced to a kind of "activity" concerned with fun, amusement, prestige value, business investment, and advertising purposes. Subjectiv*ism* reigns supreme as a person stands in front of a great painting, and art criticism is reduced to "Oh's" and "Ah's." Or art criticism is reduced to autobiographical monologues. Phrases such as "I like that," or "I don't like that," give information only about the person speaking, not about the art object. The object becomes merely the *occasion* for people to talk about themselves. And again, this is a mode of "esthetic nihilism." Self-expression can be a good, whether in the making or in the criticism of art, but the relevant issue is *what self* is being expressed. Surely, a curriculum should reflect this relevance.

Esthetics, being a synthetic theoretical discipline, will be partly constituted by the ontological. *What* the ontological is, is an ontological problem. The problem we are dealing with is the order of knowledge, and the most that can be said is *that* esthetic knowledge is partially determined by the ontological. The theory may be that art imitates the nature of things by means of the "image" or "ikon"; but, whatever it is, implicitly or explicitly, the ontological will be present. The problem of the origin and destiny of man, the nature of being and reality, cannot be ignored when considering the nature of beauty, no more so than when dealing with good and evil in ethics. As an ontological category, beauty is a unity, but has different meanings according to the different modes of its expression, e.g., pattern, design, harmony, novelty, freshness, economy, range, unity, depth.

The ontological is reflected in the history of art. Art in India cannot be understood in abstraction from Hinduism, nor can the art of the West in abstraction from the theism of the Hebraic-Christian tradition. In more recent times, the art of the Soviet Union, which has been called "social realism," cannot be understood in abstraction from dialectical materialism. In terms of the doctrinal skepticism which is subjectivism, of course there is no theological or philosophical knowledge, hence no esthetic knowledge. Therefore, in art as in morality, "it is all a matter of opinion" —which is either a trite truism or a slogan, for the pronoun "it" has no unambiguous referent.

THE USE ARTS

All of the applied sciences—engineering, technology, and agriculture—are use arts, not fine arts, for with these there is the distinction between the maker and the user, not between the maker and the experiencer. The distinction does not imply separateness. If an object can have use value and also esthetic value, then so much the better. The difference is between what is primary and what is secondary. A small transistor is made primarily for its utility, perhaps to fit into a very small space in a rocket. It might have also esthetic value, but if so that would not make it a "good" transistor from the standpoint of the engineer. An object of fine art may also have use value, but that would be accidental to its being.

What intellectual elements enter into the use arts? Being practical they are constituted by other kinds of knowledge. What are these kinds and how are they related? In what follows, "technology" will be used broadly to mean the use arts, unless in context some distinction is relevant. The following distinctions can be made which show the kinds of knowledge entering into technology: (1) the purpose for which an object is made and for which it is used; (2) the theoretical principles used in making the object; (3) the application of the principles to form the object; (4) the skill, the "know-how," in molding the raw materials into the object; (5) the art of, or skill in, using the object made. We may illustrate these by taking for analysis the construction of a bridge.

1. The purpose for which a bridge is made is economy of transportation and communication. The value is primarily economic, although there may be other values. In any case, the value is a social, a moral, one, in the sense that it is a potential good. Whether or not it becomes an actual good depends upon the specific purpose for which it is used, i.e., the purpose of the transportation. It might be built primarily for the movement of troops and materials in time of war. However, it might be for the purpose of enhancing a tyranny or of opposing it. The kind of knowledge that enters here is ethical, for technology does not determine its own ends.

2. The knowledge used in the making of the bridge will come from mathematics and the positive (experimental) sciences. These are theoretical and autonomous, we will recall, and are not practical except derivatively. They can be practical in use only because they are theoretical in nature. The physicist need not know engineering, but the engineer must know physics. Knowing how to apply physics to build bridges is not part of physics, but of engineering.

Is esthetic knowledge required in making a bridge? No, but it is desirable. Esthetic principles do not enter into technology *constitutively*, as do the principles of mathematics and physics. The engineer must know the physics of stresses and strains, otherwise the bridge will fall down and have no use value. It can have use value and yet be esthetically ugly. However, all other things being equal, the bridge should be beautiful. The qualification means that in technology use value is primary and esthetic value is secondary. The ideal is to have both. But even this ideal needs to be more carefully defined, for there is apparently no reason why, even ideally, a transistor should be beautiful. The principle for the convergence of use value and esthetic value is this, that the degree of convergence demanded is proportional to the extent that the object is experienced as well as used. Architecture is usually classified as a fine art. But in fact it is on the border line, being a sort of synthesis of fine arts and use arts. A building is constantly seen, experienced, as well as used. Hence, the demand for esthetic value as well as use value. The contrary is the case with the transistor, hence the esthetic is irrelevant.

Presumably, an elliptical curve is more pleasing to the eye than a parabolic curve. In a suspension bridge what one sees is a parabolic curve of the steel cords, and it cannot be otherwise. On the other hand, a little bridge across a small stream may be elliptical in curve, even though a parabolic arch might be less expensive and also stronger.

3. There are two kinds of "know-how" in engineering. The first kind is that of knowing how to apply the principles of mathematics and the experimental sciences to build "bridges in general." This kind of "know-how" defines an applied science, for knowing a theoretical science, though necessary, is not sufficient for the art of making. This kind of practical knowledge is the purpose for which an engineering college or institute exists, and differentiates it from a construction firm. An engineering college does not exist to build bridges, even though an actual one may be used in project work. The school teaches the "know-how" of building "bridges in general," possible bridges. The construction company exists to build an actual bridge, this particular one at this particular place, under certain specific conditions.

4. To build this or that bridge, and not bridges in general, another kind of knowledge is necessary. It is the kind that is based upon what is called "experience," and in which the theoretical element may be only implicit. This is the second kind of "know-how," and it is usually called a "skill." But it is the kind that can only be acquired by building *this* bridge, an *actual* object. This kind of skill consists in movements and manipulations based upon rules and precepts which can only *imperfectly* be communicated orally, in writing, or by imitation. This is the "know-how" of the foreman on the job. It is the technological equivalent of the moral virtue of prudence, which defines the, say, statesman rather than the mere politician. It is the art of dealing with the particular as particular. It is "on-the-job training."

5. There is finally the "art" of using the bridge, after it has been built, in an efficient manner. This is a social problem, specifically a traffic problem.

In terms of this analysis, we can now answer some questions. What is the relation between theoretical science and applied science, which is technology and is really a use art? What is the relation between both of these and the ethical?

The difference between technology and the theoretical (positive) sciences is one of instrumentality. In theoretical science, the world of material nature is instrumental to the *knowing* of the theoretical principles; in technology, the theoretical principles are instrumental in *knowing how* to *make* an object *for a purpose*. The last three words are important. In "knowing," the purpose is given, namely, to grasp the truth. It is not relative to men's interests or purposes. To put it in another way, in "knowing," the interest or purpose of seeking the truth subordinates all other interests and purposes. On the other hand, in the use arts all sorts of human purposes are relevant, for the correct "knowing how" can never be understood in abstraction from alternative purposes.

There is still another way of putting the matter. In all theoretical disciplines, philosophical or scientific, the aim is so to conduct oneself intellectually that the various patterns of order in the nature of things are impressed on the mind. The activity is, of course, a dynamic one, and the analogy of a wax impression is not implied. But it is as simple as this in principle, to use an example, that when Archimedes got to know the way solid objects behaved in fluids he framed a conceptual pattern of order which he believed to be exemplified in nature; and, if so, because of the conformity he had the truth. It was not his aim to *impose* his *own* conceptual pattern on nature, and then believe that that is the "way things are."

All art activity is just the reverse, whether it be in the fine arts or in the use arts. The aim is to *impose* a human pattern of order on material things. The purpose is making, creating; not discovery. Even if there is a sort of dialectical or causal interplay between making and discovering, so that in a carefully defined sense it can be said that one can discover through making, and make through discovering, nevertheless so far from invalidating the distinction, it is rather presupposed. In the one case man, by an act of humility, allows nature to impose her forms on his mind; in the other, man imposes his own forms, ideas, on nature. In short, the practitioner of the arts can, in a sense, "play God," and it is for this reason that he has always been tempted by pride in a way the theoretical scientist has not.

Tempted though the artist may be, and however foolish his creation may be, he really always admits the distinction between making and knowing. The painter knows that he cannot get red by mixing together yellow and green, and the physicist and chemist can tell him why. It is through *knowing* that the artist, or the technologist, respects the nature of his raw material. He knows that granite is harder than soft coal, and that as a sculptor he can make with the one what he cannot make with the other.

Let us recall that a fundamental principle of the order of knowledge is this: if one kind of knowledge is reduced to another, then both are perverted or destroyed. If either the practical or the theoretical is reduced to the other, then both vanish. This error is not committed by the artist *qua* artist, or the scientist *qua* scientist, but rather by either one if they "philosophize." Although the artist may be more tempted by pride than the scientist, yet the latter is more guilty when he succumbs. He does this when he reduces truth to "use value," or knowing to making. He knows the world he creates because he first created the world that he knows —an activity which may dignify the God of Genesis, but hardly the creature.

If both art and the moral disciplines are practical, what is the relation between them? As we have seen, technology does not furnish its own ends, for there is the knowing how to make and the knowing how to use. Technology is always on the level of "means," and as such can be used for good or for bad purposes. If used for good purposes, then it can be a moral means, for it comes under the judgment of the ethical. However, the ethical does not enter as evidence into technological knowledge, as does physics or chemistry.

With the fine arts, the matter is somewhat different. They have their own end, esthetic value. It is not furnished from without by ethics. The denial of this reduces art to a kind of moral*ism*, to the detriment of each. That a work of art has a "moral" message, or is religious, is not sufficient to make it a good work of art. On the other hand, the esthetic and the ethical are distinct; i.e., neither is reducible to the other. Nevertheless they are related, hence not separable. The relation is not direct, but one mediated by the ontological, for the ontological does enter constitutively as evidence into both esthetic and ethical principles. In the case of technology, ontological evidence does not enter in the knowing how to make; it does, however, by the way of the ethical, enter into knowing how to use. This relation is a direct one of subordination.

The order of teaching and learning must reflect these distinctions and relations in the order of knowledge. Esthetics and some practice in the fine arts is necessary in a liberal-education curriculum, as has been pointed out. Are the use arts equally necessary? No. It is difficult to see on what ground such a demand could be made. However, a case can be made for the thesis that some technological knowledge may be desirable, though not necessary. The use arts are primarily a matter of vocational and professional education. In the fine arts, esthetic value is independent of, though related to, the ethical and the religious, and because of its autonomy the esthetic must be part of a liberal education. But, in the case of the use arts, there is no such independent, autonomous value. Technology is on the level of moral means, and use value *is* a moral value, not another kind of value related to the moral. Hence, the liberal-education curriculum does not equally demand knowledge of the use arts and the fine arts.

Should the practitioner of the use arts have a liberal education? Yes, otherwise such practice may be separated from the ethical and become antisocial. For either the technologist sees his kind of knowledge in the light of the whole, or he will tend to interpret the whole in terms of the part with which he is identified, and in which case everything becomes inverted. The moral is subordinated to technique, the technological is absolutized and now becomes "technocracy," and the human being is reduced to raw material to be worked upon, a "thing" and not a "person." The "I-Thou" relationship is lost.

On the curricular level, the problem is how to bring liberal education to the student who is, or will be, studying the vocational and the professional subjects in the way of the use arts. There is a danger of confusing kinds of knowledge and getting them to compete with each other. For the purpose of illustration, we have already referred to the "bridge engineer." Using it again, we may say that both the curriculum and the teachers will not confuse (a) what constitutes engineering as a practical discipline; (b) what the engineer *qua* engineer must know; and finally, (c) what knowledge is desirable for a man to have who happens to be an engineer? With these distinctions in mind, the words of a famous engineer can better be understood.

Contrary to the popular conception, the calculation of stresses and sections, the designing of members and details, and the supervision of their erection are not the only things a bridge engineer has to do. In addition, he has to conceive a project, develop it, verify and demonstrate its economic justification, battle opposition and secure authorization, wrestle with problems of legislation and financing, determine the best location from both engineering and city-planning considerations, determine the best type and layout for economy, efficiency, and durability, place approaches and connections for maximum convenience and safety of traffic, design the form, lines, and proportions of the structure for beauty as well as for strength, select and specify the best materials for the work, prepare construction contracts and specification, deal with public officials, property owners, clients, contractors, and material men, present recommendations and reports in a clear and convincing style, and—above all— have a sound and comprehensive grasp of the civic and social import and influence of his plan.[2]

---

[2] The quotation is taken from the book *The Builders of the Bridge*, by V. B. Steinmann, and is found in a review of the book in *Saturday Review of Literature*, May 12, 1945.

5

THE CURRICULUM AND EFFICIENT CAUSATION

There are many efficient causes in the teaching-learning activity, one of the most important being the curriculum. A curriculum is a plan of study, or studies, and is a means used by the teacher in helping the student to learn. The importance of the curriculum lies in this, that through it the school expresses its actual meaning and purpose—actual, in contrast to the verbal utterances of an administrator, or, say, the self-given eulogies to be found in a college catalogue or brochure.

In order to understand the nature of a curriculum as one of the causes whereby the student learns, two questions must be asked. What are the determinants that constitute any given curriculum? And how does each do so? And let us remember that a curriculum is a means, hence a human construct.

There are many means, but the relevant distinction for the problem at hand is between the necessary and the accidental. In the teaching-learning activity the teacher is a means, certainly not an end. From the standpoint of the student the teacher is a means of helping him get to know something. And the teacher must also so conceive of himself; for that is precisely what defines him as a teacher, and not merely a neighbor, an acquaintance, etc.

The other necessary means is a plan of studies, a curriculum, for without it a teacher could not teach. The necessity lies in the teaching activity, and not in the relative awareness of the teacher. The teacher may not know, in a theoretical way, what a curriculum is, and it may be well or poorly organized. In any case, he will have one, for a curriculum has to be a curriculum in order to be appraised as good, bad, chaotic, etc.

Of course, even among necessary means, perhaps the most important of the efficient causes in the order of teaching and learning is the student himself. One of the characteristics that distinguish persons from other creatures is the teaching-learning activity, and in this respect there is an existential identity of material and efficient causes. The person who is taught *must* also teach himself. Otherwise, there would only be *conditioning*; neither teaching nor learning in the *human* sense. In fact, without exaggeration it may be said that the teacher, as an efficient cause, causes the student to become his own efficient cause in learning. The student is always a relatively potential efficient cause. The function of the teacher is to help actualize what is potential. In doing this, one of the necessary means is the curriculum.

The accidental means in the teaching-learning activity are many and varied, depending upon the existential circumstances under which such activity takes place. Examples are books (remote teachers), buildings, chairs, tables, chalk, blackboard, pencils, pens, teaching-machines, movies, television, tapes, visits to factories and museums, and countless others. None of these is necessary to teaching *qua* teaching, for such activity went on in history long before any of these helpful artifacts existed. It is important to recognize the distinction between what is necessary and what is desirable. What is necessary is that which is intrinsic to teaching, that which makes it *what* it is, whether or not it is effective or ineffective. What is desirable is that which makes for effective teaching and learning. Teaching has to be *what* it is, independent of the "desirable," in order that *it* can be appraised.

It is for this reason that the essence of, the intrinsic nature of, the teaching-learning acticity can be dealt with, as we are doing, independent of the existential conditions in different times and places. However, such conditions are relevant in determining this or that *particular* teaching-learning activity as relatively effective or ineffective.

Although these distinctions may be recognized, yet their significance may remain obscured. When that happens differences may arise between educators because a partial truth is taken as the whole truth. Such a quarrel took place some years ago—and unfortunately, still continues—between Robert Hutchins, then President of the University of Chicago, and the so-called "Progressivists" in education. For illustration and analysis we may give two quotations:

Education implies teaching, teaching implies knowledge. Knowledge is truth. The truth is everywhere the same . . . I suggest that the heart of any course of study designed for the whole people will be, if education is rightly understood, the same at any time, in any place, under any political, social, or economic conditions.[1]

Being a form of social action, education always has a geographical and cultural location; it is therefore specific, local, and dynamic, not general, universal, and unchanging; it is a function of a particular society at a particular time and place in history; it is rooted in some actual culture and expresses the philosophy and recognized needs of that culture.[2]

Now, properly interpreted, each quotation is saying something that is true. But, unfortunately, there was not the proper inter-

---

[1] Robert M. Hutchins, *The Higher Learning in America*, New Haven: Yale University Press, 1936, p. 66.
[2] American Historical Association, *Report of the Commission of Social Studies: Conclusions and Recommendations*, New York: Charles Scribner's Sons, 1934, p. 31.

pretation, for both parties confused the distinction between knowledge and curricular categories, between the order of knowledge and the order of teaching and learning.

Mr. Hutchins' critics usually attacked the notion that "the truth is everywhere the same." They missed the essential point. For, even if this is granted—and would one wish completely to deny it?—it does not follow that all courses of study must be the same. Why? Because, as we shall see later through analysis, what determines a curriculum, a "course of study," is not the same as that which determines truth and knowledge. Mr. Hutchins' error was to try to do that which is impossible, namely, to deduce the order of teaching and learning from the order of knowledge.

On the other hand, the Report of the American Historical Association stresses the relativity of the curriculum, any given curriculum being a function of many variables, two of which are time and place. All of which is correct in emphasis against such an error as Mr. Hutchins made. But the "Report" gives the impression that the emphasis is absolutized, in which case an equally fatal error is made. For it would seem that time and place now become such "constants" that knowledge, truth, as one determinant among others, is overlooked. If so, then not only the curriculum, but even knowledge itself becomes a function of a given culture; and this would, *even though not intentionally meant*, reduce teaching to some kind of "ideological determination." In short, this error is that of supposing that the order of knowledge can be deduced from curricular categories.

The historians who wrote the "Report" would probably be the first to admit that truth is the "same everywhere"—or should be—when it comes to a thousand and one propositions, from those of mathematics to those of ethics, e.g., that the person should be respected, not exploited, etc. And Mr. Hutchins, undoubtedly, if the matter were clarified for him, would admit that the curriculum is a variable, and cannot be the same "everywhere." In short, there is that in education which is necessary and desirable (hence constant) and that which is relatively desirable but not necessary (hence variable).

What are the determinants that constitute a curriculum, *anywhere and at any time?* The answer may be seen by examining the summary formula of the teaching-learning activity: T teaches K to S, by (means of) M, and for (the purpose) E. The curriculum (C), being a necessary means which is also a human construct, is determined by T, K, S, and E, and in what follows there will be an analysis of how each factor determines.

First, however, it may be noted that, although C is one "M" among others, it is unique. The teacher is a necessary means, but not a human construct. A tape recorder is a human construct that may be desirable, but is not absolutely necessary. A curriculum, on the other hand, is a human construct that is desirable because it is necessary.

Any given curriculum will be determined by the purpose for which the teacher teaches and the student learns. Since, as we have seen in an earlier chapter, there are immediate and remote ends, there will be constant as well as variable factors. Without exception, the immediate end for both the student and the teacher is that of having the student get to know something. Granting that there is an intrinsic value in learning for learning's sake, nevertheless the question can be asked—learn for what purpose? The purposes may be many—to work in a machine shop, to get a liberal education, to become a lawyer, etc. However, it is neither possible nor desirable to have a different curriculum for the countless different purposes. Therefore, a curriculum will in practice be determined by certain broad categories—elementary, secondary, college, and university. A constant factor throughout all these levels will be the curricular expression of "liberal education," although the mode and manner of accomplishing this will vary. A secondary school or a Junior College may have a "terminal" curriculum, as well as others; and there are all the special cases, e.g., for retarded children, the handicapped, etc.

The constant factors in any curriculum should be, then, the immediate end, that of getting to know something, and secondly, that of liberal education. The latter is necessary because it perfects one in becoming human, and the student is first of all a human being.

How does the teacher function as a determinant in a program of studies, or in a "course"? The course or program of studies as *actually taught*, in contrast with the "ideal" curriculum as advertised by the school, will depend upon the knowledge and goodwill of the teacher. Even the ideal curriculum, printed and advertised by the school, represents of necessity a selection of materials within the kind of knowledge being taught. The teacher will further select, or may make additions, for he would be an automaton if he did not. To the degree that he lacks knowledge of his "subject," he may leave out important aspects about which he knows little, e.g., an "older" mathematics teacher who does not understand "sets," etc. Worse still, a teacher may attempt to teach what he does not know because he may be unaware of his ignorance. The selection and addition of materials also depends upon the goodwill, the good faith, of the teacher. A course on the Civil War in the United States may, if taught by one who loves his fellow men because they are human beings, be quite different from the "same" course taught by another teacher who has an anti-Negro bias.

It is obvious that the nature of the student being taught will determine, in part, any given curriculum; for, after all, it is for the student that the curriculum exists. The relevant factors will be the student's age, his environment, and his capacity. The causal relations between the student and the curriculum may be stated in four propositions:

1. As the student changes, so must the curriculum.

2. The converse also is possible, for through proper change in a curriculum the student may more efficiently learn.

3. As the student changes, knowledge does *not* necessarily change. What might change, however, is the student's way of knowing.

4. If knowledge changes, it is possible to effect a change in the student. Knowledge can change in two ways. First, there can be such an accumulation of data and theory on a line that the limited truths of the past take on new meanings. An example of this would be the recent "knowledge explosion" in the physical sciences. Second, there can be a change in depth in knowledge. An example of this would be the increasing understanding, historically, of the nature and application of natural rights; that such rights were held not only by the slave owners but by the slaves themselves; hence that slavery is unjust.

THE INTENTIONALITY OF THE CURRICULUM

A little linguistic analysis may be helpful in understanding what the curriculum is and what it is not, although language in itself cannot be a sufficient explanation.

Both orally and in writing there is an economy in the use of language. It is well that this is so, provided the distinction between language and that which is meant is not erased. A complete sentence may be an incomplete proposition, e.g., "Caesar crossed the Rubicon." This is a complete sentence, but not a complete historical proposition; for he could not cross "in general." To be complete, at the minimum, there would have to be added "at a given place and at a given time," with the place and time specified. We express ourselves also in incomplete arguments, allowing, as in the case of the incomplete proposition, the context to supply what is necessary. A person may say, "you'll die one of these days; after all, you're human." What is assumed, but left unsaid, is that "all human beings will die."

We have already pointed out this economy in language in analyzing the teaching relation. A person may say "I teach John." Literally, this is impossible. What is really meant is, "I am a teacher of John" or "I teach John mathematics, or geography, etc.," i.e., some kind of knowledge.

Now, let us suppose a teacher in grade six, says, "I am teaching Australia today." This again, is a manner of speaking, for literally it is impossible. Only knowledge can be taught and Australia is not knowledge, but rather is an existential name or category. What the teacher means to say is that he intends to teach knowledge *about* Australia. "Australia" is an existential category (not concept) that is used as a curricular instrument for integrating and for the purpose of learning various kinds of knowledge. The teacher will bring into his teaching some economics, meteorology, sociology, geography, and geology. In this way the student will get to know not only *that* the people in Australia once exported sheep primarily, rather than corn or wheat, but also, because of meteorological knowledge, he will understand *why*.

An emergent fact in this analysis, and a very important one indeed, is that a curricular category need not be a knowledge category. The word "chemistry" may stand for a kind of knowledge or "a course." To say that a person teaches a course in chemistry is a manner of speaking. What is literally meant is that he teaches chemistry, a kind of knowledge. "Course" is a curricular category, referring to some *ordered means by which* he teaches such knowledge. One really cannot teach "a course"; rather one teaches a kind of knowledge for which the "course" is a means. On the other hand, an existential category such as "Australia" can not be taught at all for it is not a knowledge category. One can only teach about Australia, whereas the chemistry teacher teaches chemistry and not about chemistry, except incidentally. Likewise, a student cannot "learn Australia," he can only learn *about* Australia. But one can say that a student learns chemistry, and not merely learns about it.

If so, then a nonknowledge category such as "Australia" can be a curricular means of learning and teaching and in two ways. First, the student gets to know something about existence, the world in which he lives. He does not merely get an abstract form of knowledge for the sake of getting the knowledge. Second, in the activity of getting to know something about Australia he is encouraged by his teacher to learn a little of the nonexistential, i.e., those kinds of knowledge such as economics, meteorology, etc. In fact, he *must* do the second if he is to accomplish the first.

Here we see the truth in the "project method" advocated by, and usually associated with—though not necessarily so—those concerned with what had been called "progressive education." The protest which was quite justified, as we shall soon see, was against an excessive "intellectualism" in education. However, without further analysis, this truth may not be at all obvious. A further clarification of the difference between existential and knowledge categories is necessary.

Relevant to our analysis is the distinction between "propositions of" and "propositions about." There can only be propositions *about* singular existents—and every existent is a "singular." Without prejudicing, for the moment the question of whether or not "God exists," there can be no propositions *of* God, only propositions *about* God. There can be no propositions of human beings, propositions of electrons, only propositions about human beings and about electrons. However, when one comes to the nonexistential, the matter is different. In considering knowledge, or kinds of knowledge, there can be propositions *both* of and about. The proposition, "when hydrochloric acid and sodium sulfate are mixed (under given conditions), sulfuric acid and sodium chloride are produced," is a proposition *of* chemistry. The proposition, "Chemistry is a very important science in the promotion of human welfare," is a proposition *about* chemistry. It is not at all a proposition of chemistry, but rather an appraisal of chemistry as a kind of knowledge. In fact, any proposition having "chemistry" as the subject *cannot* be a proposition of chemistry; it must be *about* it. This holds true for every kind of knowledge, with but one exception, philosophy. The reason for the exception is this, that knowledge about knowledge is itself a kind of knowledge, and hence a proposition *about* philosophy can be, and may be in certain cases, a proposition of philosophy.

In summation: (1) A "proposition of" can only refer to a proposition in some kind of knowledge; (2) a "proposition *about*" can refer to (a) a kind of knowledge, (b) general statements about existents, or (c) a statement about some specific singular existent, e.g., John Jones, God, *this* blade of grass, etc. Note should be taken of the fact that when the teacher teaches about Australia, no amount of knowledge from all the sciences is sufficient to grasp, in understanding, the very *being* of Australia. As a singular existent, it transcends, in its *being*, all propositions *about* it. Also, the kinds of knowledge introduced by the teacher for the understanding of Australia, e.g., meteorology, economics, etc., transcend as knowledge the limited existent which is Australia. In fact, their value as knowledge lies in the fact that they are relatively independent of the existent, Australia, and *hence* can be useful in the understanding of that specific existential entity.

THE RELEVANCE TO TEACHING AND LEARNING

The distinction between curricular and knowledge categories, and that between "propositions of" and "propositions about," is of great importance in throwing light on certain past and present educational problems. Those who stressed "doing" in learning have been opposed by those who have stressed "knowing." The latter have been accused of conceiving of the student as a sort of disembodied mind which is to be developed through various forms of "mental exercises." The former have been accused of conceiving of the student as essentially a material being which, to be developed, had to undergo ceaseless physical behavior. The alternatives seemed to be either to learn by knowing or to learn by doing, and the tendency was to reduce the one to the other. "Learning by doing" became a battle slogan. When each is taken in opposition to the other, like typical contraries, both cannot be true. However, both can be false; but so often the protagonists saw only, yet correctly, the falsity of the opposing position.

The truth is, we suggest, that both doing and learning are instrumental to the other. One reason this was not always understood was the confusion in the matter of priority, the psychological and the logical. The human being is first of all an experiencer, and knowledge emerges. With the exception of revelation from God, if this be granted, all knowledge comes with and from sense experience. This is the truth, if only partial, of what has been called the "empiricist doctrine." Through reflection on experience, various kinds of knowledge are obtained. In turn, the knowledge is applied to new experiences. Causally speaking, there is an interplay between sense and intellectual activity. If justice is not done to the intellectual, the human being tends to be reduced to his animal nature. If justice is not done to sense experience, the human being suffers another kind of reduction, that to pure spirit, to the purely rational. Each reductionist position, being absolutized, becomes an "ism," empiricism and rationalism.

Much of educational theory and practice in modern times has, unfortunately, reflected these two positions, giving rise to really unnecessary quarrels. The ontological basis of the reductionism can be traced back at least to the contradictions and difficulties of Cartesianism. The duality of body and mind, the physical and mental, became a dual*ism*. After various unsuccessful attempts to put back together that which Descartes had rent asunder, philosophers tended toward simpler ways out, namely, to reduce the one to the other. This gave rise in modern times to what has been called spiritualism or idealism, on the one hand, and materialism or naturalism, on the other. The former, then, in educational theory tends to emphasize the knowing peculiar to man, those kinds of abstraction that only the intellect can perform. Unfortunately, this position was enhanced by the rise of modern mathematics, which requires a high degree of abstraction. The nature of the error was the attempt to reduce all kinds of abstract knowledge to a mathematical model. This almost defines modern rationalism. On the other hand, the latter position emphasized interaction with the environment, since man is primarily a bio-social creature in the existential context of nature alone. And, of course, "interaction" is both "doing" and "being acted upon."

The notion of "doing" became, for educational purposes, further delimited in terms of materialism or naturalism. The proper kind of doing is "adjustment," the improper kind leads to "maladjustment." The proper kind is that which is done "scientifically." This kind of doing also implies that to be scientific one must act scientifically, and such action has as its aim "changing the world." And this demands "manipulation" of things. If it is done in the manner of the scientific method, then it is done correctly. All else is magic, superstition, etc. One "knows" when one is "doing" or acting in a scientific manner. Although there is no longer any immaterial "intellect," nevertheless there is "intelligence." In fact, it is found throughout nature, and is not peculiar to man. What is unique to man is the fact that, so far as the evidence is concerned, he is the most intelligent creature. The lower the scale of life the more a living entity must adapt to nature. With the coming of man, and his discovery of the scientific method, a converse kind of activity is relatively intensified. For now man adapts nature to his own purposes and interests. To the extent that he is relatively successful, he shows the mark of intelligence. He knows how to manipulate things, and in the process of so doing he also learns. In fact, the proper knowing is a kind of doing; for "intelligence" becomes adjectival to the body.

If one believes that this simplistic position does justice neither to the nature of man nor to the activities of teaching and learning, he is probably correct. The educational implications are deductions from an assumed ontological position—assumed because contemporary naturalism and materialism are postulated and not argued. But it is useless to oppose this position by offering another error, if error it be, namely, an excessive intellectualism. There is a great deal of truth in the naturalistic or materialistic position regarding human intelligence, and especially in some of its implications as to pedagogical procedure. The most efficacious criticism is that it is not the whole truth, which is its essential claim, and further that it does not do justice to all of the facts of the teaching-learning activities.

There are two meanings of "doing" in relation to knowing. To learn anything one must do something. One must do mathematics in order to know it. One must do metaphysics in order to know it. And so on, for physics, chemistry, etc. These kinds of knowledge are on a highly abstract level, but they require a "doing" just as much as does "on-the-job training," when one learns how to repair automobile engines. Of course, it is a different kind of "doing"; in fact, so much so that there is almost a "play" upon the word. In kinds of knowledge of a high degree of abstraction "doing" refers, not to conduct, but rather to that kind of intellectual activity which is *knowing* itself. Doing mathematics *is* getting to know it. Doing is then a synonym for knowing.

In the sense in which doing and knowing are not synonymous, in the sense in which there is a *conceptual* difference, doing refers to human conduct. It is in this sense that, *really* being different, doing and knowing are each instrumental to the other. Theoretical knowing is the result of methods of abstraction by which the general and the universal are obtained from particular sense experience. The sense experience comes first, and it is always of particulars. One may seek knowledge of a universal kind about trees, but one can only sense this or that tree, or a group of them. It is *this* electron that one looks at (though a streak it may be) in the photograph. One cannot see or photograph electrons in general. One begins with the particular, rises to the general and universal, and then brings to bear the latter on particular experience again. One cannot get to know merely by contemplating the Platonic heavens.

In the learning process this priority of the particular experience is a psychological one. But one *senses* the existential, or some aspect of the existential; the *conceptual* can not be sensed as such. Hence, on the pedagogical level the psychological and the existential are peculiarly linked together. But only on that level, and this is an important fact to understand, for this association does not hold at all on the level of knowledge alone. The cardinal number system is what it is independently of whether or not these or those items exist which are countable. But it does not at all follow that in the activity of teaching and learning such logical priority must be carried over into pedagogy. Although *what* is taught is mathematics, it is *to* the student; and *how* it is taught depends in part on the nature of the student. The teacher may manipulate apples that are countable, or set up a store in the back of the classroom as a project so that the students can learn their numbers by buying or selling. What is pedagogically best is not the problem here. The point is that from the standpoint of the curricular, and hence, pedagogical level, there is the priority of the existential and the psychological over the logical and the conceptual. This can be illustrated in many ways, and here is another example. Logically, on the level of knowledge alone, a profound knowledge of biology implies some knowledge of chemistry. If a student refuses for some reason to learn chemistry, then the school has the right to refuse to let him pursue a degree in biology. All of this has nothing whatsoever to do with psychology, whether it be that of the student or of the teachers. From this, however, it does not follow that on another level or order, that of pedagogy, that the same priority can be deduced for the curriculum. It may be wise first to introduce the student to the existential world of living things which are the most concrete to him, and which are of the greatest interest to him. The student experiences frogs, cats, etc., and not, say, carbon. As the student's motivation is increased by an appeal to the more existential, then the teacher can show him why, if he is serious about understanding the nature of life, a knowledge of chemistry is necessary.

There are the knowledge and curricular levels of order. The fundamental principle is that priorities may be reversed if there is a change in the standpoint of orders. The two ways of denying this principle are that of the reduction of the one to the other, or the other to the one. And, of course, historically this has been done. As we have pointed out before, the protagonist of each kind of reduction quite correctly sees the falsity of the opposite position. But both are false. If this has not always been perceived it is partially because the twentieth century has been witness, in teacher education, to an overemphasis on the "psychology of education."

The project method recognizes the mutual instrumentality of doing and knowing, and it does so for very good reasons. In the first place, there is nothing wrong in itself in going on field trips, visiting factories, going to slum areas, etc. The real existential world in which the student lives contains just these things, and many more. How can the student learn *about* such things if he has not first *experienced* them? We tread on dangerous ground here, for a false if not absurd interpretation can be put upon this. It may be pointed out that no progress could be made from generation to generation if each had to repeat all the experiences of the former. Isn't the whole aim of education to learn *from* the experience of those of the past without having to repeat all their experiences, including their errors? Of course, the answer must be in the affirmative if the question is put in this way. Certainly one does not experimentally have to be a fool or a coward first in order to understand the virtue of courage. It is not necessary to practice superstitions first in order to later discover the genius of the scientific method. No, to put it bluntly and crudely, it is wise pedagogy for the student to be made to learn, by the present teacher or the remote teacher—a textbook, perhaps—something about the nature of fire and burning. It would be educationally foolish to insist that the student must stick his hand in the fire and get burnt in order to understand.

Those who have insisted upon such an interpretation have given "educationists" a bad name. But there is such a type of "mind," and often they have appropriated to themselves the word "liberal." It seems, according to them, that "everything" in the way of man's knowledge and experience is "open to question." In their writings the word "experimental" and "creative" suffer in meaning from constant repetition. It rarely occurs to these people that such words can be used as substitutes for thought, and not necessarily as a reflection of thinking. Disagreement with them means only one thing, that one is "dogmatic" and "closed-minded." Perhaps what is relevant here is the old saying to the effect that it is good to be open-minded—open at one end and shut at the other; if open at both ends, there is only a draft.

Why continually pursue truth and certainty, if it can never be obtained in any respect? It is no answer at all to say that one must be satisfied with constantly approaching certainty. In a sense, this is correct. But it can hardly be the whole story, for unless there was certainty in some respect one could not know that in other respects one was truly approaching it.

What the project method—in fact, all learning by doing—assumes is that the student most efficiently learns when he begins with the actual, concrete experience of the singular existents in the world—not only the existential situations that are by accident part of his geographical or local experience, but also those determined by the teachers and the school which, having the responsibility and power earned by merit, have the moral right to make such decisions. The student is in school to learn, and not to teach the teachers.

That knowing, in turn, is instrumental to doing needs no comment. The relation of means and ends is reversed. But what needs to be noted is a possible error; in fact an actual error committed by some educational theorists in the name of the project method. It is one thing to go to a factory or to a slum area; it is quite different, in the name of "doing," to make the factory products or to organize ways to eliminate the slum area. This holds true for all levels of education, but especially for elementary and secondary education. It is not the function of the school to become a substitute for a social organization or a business organization, for then the uniqueness of the school is lost. The little store in the back of the classroom in an early grade is not a real one for business purposes; nor are the apples grown in an agricultural college. These schools are concerned *primarily* with knowing, and *secondarily* with doing as instrumental.

All of this is quite compatible with the notion that students should be active in an extracurricular way. After studying slums for the purpose of knowing about them, the student may be encouraged to *do* something about them. But if so, he does it as a person, as a citizen, etc., but not as a student *qua* student. Likewise, distinction between what is primary and what is secondary is not broken down by college programs, found in some engineering schools, in which the student studies in school for a certain length of time and for an equal length of time works in a factory or some business concern. Rather the very nature of the program reflects the distinction. Without the distinction, the uniqueness of the institutions is lost, precisely because the primary purpose of each is blurred.

Those who have committed the error have tended to reduce the school to an ideological instrument of social change. It has been said: "The school is as large as life itself; the school should be concerned with the *whole* person." The implications are, more often implicit than explicit, that the school should gradually take over the function of the home and the church. Insofar as these slogans are true, they are truisms; otherwise they are false, and dangerously so, for it is a totalitarian doctrine. If one wishes to hold such a position, he may do so, but in so doing he is denying the primary function of the school. The position does not arise out of any necessity in the order of teaching and learning. Rather, it denies the order by turning education into a propaganda instrument. Social change is desirable, but if it is to be rational and intelligible it will require the uniqueness of the school, which is concerned *primarily* with teaching and learning. Otherwise, a kind of antiteaching and antilearning will produce only social "flux."

Parenthetically, it may be remarked that the distinctions and principles we have made hold for *all* education and not just some, e.g., what in the United States are called "public schools." To be specific, they hold also for Catholic, Jewish, or other parochial schools. The reason for this is that the principles and distinctions made are discoverable on the order of teaching and learning activities. They are not just deductions from an ontological position. In a Catholic school, for example, in an arithmetic class there is nothing wrong, for example, in using rosary beads to learn the numbers. But the primary purpose must be to learn arithmetic, and not merely make more devout Catholics. The two purposes need not conflict if neither one is made a substitute for the other. Otherwise, contrary to what Catholicism professes to be, it becomes ideological. And some Catholic critics, themselves, have said that this sometimes happens.

There is a second reason for the recognition of the mutual instrumentality of doing and knowing in pedagogical procedures. Expressed in ontological terms, the principle is that of the priority of existence over essence. However, the principle is not an arbitrary assumption; it has an experiential foundation which has been recognized in the teaching activity.

The term "experience" far transcends the conceptual. However, knowledge that is conceptual, a product of a high degree of abstraction, is unique to man. Other animals may be said to "know," if knowing is carefully interpreted in an analogical way. Certainly one dog can be said to know another dog. A dog makes distinctions between dogs and other things, and also between male and female dogs. Human beings act similarly. But dogs or other animals do not create concepts, propositions, arguments, and by intellectual abstraction construct different kinds of knowledge. Yet, these animals can be said to come into contact with existents and experience them. A dog may not know what a human being is, or what human nature is, but it can be said to know its master in contrast to a stranger. This is a matter of evidence, regardless of linguistic expression. Hence, since a human being is *first* of all an animal, however much more he may be potentially, human *experience is* not only prior to the conceptual, but is also much more extensive. The human being has feelings and emotions, likes and dislikes, etc.; he is not merely a "knowing entity" on a conceptual level.

By means of concepts we can grasp and come to know the essential nature of a thing. The truth of this statement is independent of any particular notion of "essence." Whether essential natures are "eternal," or a set of "dispositional properties" confined at most to some historical epoch, is a metaphysical problem. But unless concepts have some foundation in the nature of things, there could be no conceptual knowledge. In addition to essence there is the act of existence, which makes anything *this* and not *that*. The act of existence makes for uniqueness and singularity. A particular person, John Jones, has an essential human nature. But so do other human beings. What makes John Jones just that person, and not someone else, is his act of existing, for he is not an abstract essence floating around in a possible world. The same holds true for a blade of grass, or any singular thing in nature; and everything in nature is singular, for universal concepts have only mental being.

Essence and existence are correlative terms. Each has meaning only in terms of the other. When one tries to know *what* things are, there is the struggle to acquire a *real*, and not merely nominal, definition. This would be impossible without abstraction and the formation of concepts. However, the essential nature of any finite thing is not only the capacity to be, to exist, but is also by that very fact a principle of limitation. That which makes existence possible is also that which delimits the kind and mode of existence. If there were no essential natures, there would be nothing to receive the act of existence. There would only be the act of pure existence, which in fact is what God is supposed to be. Whether or not God exists is not now the issue. In any case, there could not be a world of finite things. On the other hand, if there were *only* essential natures, there would only be possible worlds. Without the act of existence, there could be no actual world of finite things. Furthermore, it is the act of existence which is the basis of all dynamism and creative energy. In abstraction from existence essences are passive. They become merely the content of concepts, and nothing is so passive as a concept. Even the concept of the "dynamic" is not itself a dynamic concept.

What is the relevance of all of this to doing and knowing? Conceptual knowing, which is theoretical knowledge, is limited to the grasping of the essential nature of things. But existence as such cannot be conceptually grasped in the same way, for the act of existence is something over and above essence. Most important of all, existence is not just another essence. Hence, to know the actual existing world conceptual knowing is necessary but not sufficient. How, then, is the existential to be encountered and known by the student? *Not* by intellectual activity alone; for while this is necessary, it is not sufficient. To hold otherwise is to fall into the error of excessive intellectualism in education. The teacher, through constant talking (conceptualizing), and by means of textbooks (remote teachers), is supposed to pour universal truths into the "mind" of the student.

What else can be done? What alternatives are there? Doing is instrumental to knowing in two ways. First, as has already been shown, a certain amount of doing is necessary even for the kind of knowing that is conceptual abstraction. Second, doing is necessary to obtain knowledge over and above the conceptual, that knowledge which a person can have only because he acts as a *whole* being in relation to other existents, human and nonhuman. His action is conduct, it is doing and not merely intellectual activity. It has been called knowledge "by acquaintance with." A person knows his family and friends, his town or city, by acting. There is the existential encounter of one person with the other. Likewise, one can get to know the particular things in nature through existential encounter. John Jones knows *this* tree in front of *this* house on *this* bit of land. Intellectually John Jones can learn about human nature, about trees, about land, etc., but all this is something quite different. The existential encounter—and at least some knowledge by acquaintance was acquired—took place *before* he became a student. If it were not so, there would be nothing *in his experience* for the teacher to appeal to.

Neither kind of knowledge can be a substitute for the other. They are complementary. Moreover, the knowledge the student gets by *doing*, before he goes to school, does not cease at the time he goes to school. It continues throughout his lifetime. The student climbs a mountain, and his experience is so exhilarating that he writes a poem about it. His doing leads him to obtain knowledge through poetic experience. Just *what* he knows is not at issue here, and in any case it may be difficult to define. But there would not be even this problem were it not the case that he knows something. It is in this sense that one may be said to know through poetry. Needless to say, this truth can be and has been abused. The point to be made is that, whatever it may be that he knows through such an existential encounter with a bit of nature, it was something that he acquired by *doing*, by acting as a whole human being. It could never be acquired by conceptual abstraction, by studying books about mountains, or by listening to a teacher's lectures about such. Hence, there is a great deal of difference between the doing which is merely intellectual activity, i.e., studying books about mountains and mountain climbing, and the kind of doing which is an existential encounter with reality, in this case climbing a mountain. The latter may inspire poetic experience, the former does not.

To sum up, doing is instrumental to knowing not only in the sense of "conceptual knowing"; it is also instrumental to nonconceptual knowing, that which comes from *experience with*, or acquaintance with, existence.

At this point some caveats are necessary. The term "experience" can be very vague, and it can be used to cover up problems as well as to help solve them. The philosophy of John Dewey cannot be dismissed as wholly false. He was trying to say something that needed to be said. Nevertheless, he can legitimately be criticized in his use of the word "experience," which became for him almost the equivalent of the metaphysical term "being." Perhaps this can be explained in terms of his early Hegelianism. Nevertheless, cannot one say that the experience of a tree is an experience?—in which case one has said nothing. It is something quite different to speak of a tree as "experience," and then argue that since a tree is "objective" therefore experience is objective. This was so explicit in Dewey that A. N. Whitehead, following Dewey, was forced to give it all a metaphysical foundation in his work, *Process and Reality*. In fact, a tree became a "democracy." Technically, this is called "Pan-psychism." What is questionable, however, is the politicizing of metaphysics, which tends toward ideology, not philosophy, and which is something radically different from the metaphysical or ontological basis of democracy. The defense of democracy, in any reasonable sense, on a social level for human beings does not at all require its highly questionable ontological extension to all of being and reality. The assumption that it does offers reasonable grounds for the critics of Dewey to the effect that, under the guise of educational philosophy, he was actually putting forth an ideology which would reduce the school essentially to an instrument of social change. In fairness to Dewey, however, it may be that such criticism should be directed toward some of his followers who spoke in his name. In fact, before his death, he hinted the same.

Keeping in mind the danger in the use of the term "experience," what can be meant by "existential experience" in contrast to "conceptual experience"? All experience can be traced to two sources, sense experience and revelation from God. If God does not exist, then there is only the former. On this no one will disagree. The reasonable naturalist or materialist does not deny the possibility of revealed truth *if* God exists. He denies the possibility of revelation—and quite logically in a formal sense—*because* God does not exist. Let us, therefore, limit ourselves to the former, sense experience. This will be sufficient for our purpose, and it would be misleading to rest our case upon the latter.

"Sense experience" is to be interpreted very broadly, for there is no reason, for the purpose of our analysis, arbitrarily to restrict it. Not merely colors, sounds, etc., or the "five senses," is meant. It is through sense experience, in part, that a man knows *his* wife and children—not about wives in general, or about marriage in general, or about children in general. This holds true for any person, and the student is a person. Such experience or knowledge can only be acquired by dynamic and creative *doing* on the part of a person, and therefore on the part of the student *qua* student. Just as existence transcends essence, so sense experience of the existent world transcends conceptual experience. Sense experience is much more inclusive, and it is from such experience that conceptual experience is obtained by a process of abstraction. Hence, doing, i.e., the act of human existence, is necessary for and instrumental to knowing.

The Marxist materialist has always recognized this truth. The

Communist cadre is never "educated" by merely reading about dialectic materialism or about worker's problems. He will understand the worker's problems when he *does* something, i.e., participates actively in the class struggle. This fact, however, does not prove Marxism or dialectic materialism. For the argument is: if Marxism, this is true; it does not follow that if this is true, hence Marxism. This has been recognized in many ways and has been expressed in many statements. A person may say: "If you want to know what it is like to have a black skin, darken yours and live in a Negro section of a city." Again: "If a student is to become a professor of economics, he ought to spend a year stooping in a coal mine, or some equivalent."

It has been pointed out before, and should be mentioned again, that all this does not mean that one must actively seek each and every kind of experience. It is true that doing is instrumental to, and necessary for, learning; but it is a mark of wisdom on the part of the teacher to know what kind of doing is to be encouraged and what is not. Otherwise one would have to murder in order to know what a murderer is, etc.

For finite things in this world the distinction between essence and existence does not mean separation. There is no pure existence in this world without essence, and there are no essential natures floating around in this world without existence. Likewise, sense experience and conceptual experience can be distinguished, but not separated. A person does not live, having only sense experience—that would be an animal kind of existence. Nor does one live merely in a conceptual world. The conceptual is always found in sense experience, and sense experience is always found in the conceptual. Each is instrumental to the other, although sense experience is prior to and transcends the conceptual just as there is the priority of existence over essence. Hence, it can be said, if very carefully interpreted, that there is a priority of doing over knowing. Insofar as Dewey and his followers, those who have been called "progressive educationists," have asserted this thesis they have been correct as against those in educational theory who have been called "essentialists." It also marks the truth of the "existentialist" emphasis in recent educational theory.

Creative teaching and creative learning are mutually implicatory. Both are dynamic. The proper type of curriculum cannot be confined to knowing alone, leaving all doing to extra-curricular activities. A curriculum will be planned for both, and yet, the correct instrumental relation must be observed; otherwise the uniqueness, in fact the essential nature of the school, is lost. To put it in an illustrative form, for the student in school doing is instrumental to getting to know. When the same person is out of school working, say, as a physician, then knowing is instrumental to doing. The uniqueness, the very essence of institutional education is also its limitation. The school, like any other institution, is limited in its purpose and function. It cannot be otherwise. It is one thing to say that there should be cooperation between the school, home, and church. It is something quite different to attempt the impossible and maintain that the school should take over the functions of the other two. This is a recipe for the destruction of all three, which is only consistent with a political absolutism or some other form of social totalitarianism. The priority of parental rights over school "rights" is not an arbitrary principle at all. Rather, it is a built-in necessity in the activities that constitute the order of teaching and learning, and not at all a deduction from an ontological position arbitrarily postulated.

It may seem that in relating doing and knowing, and existence and essence, we have taken an excursion into the realm of the ontological, and therefore have abandoned the phenomenological approach in which we describe "what is there." It is true that we have used the ontological categories, essence and existence. But the same approach has been carried over in the analysis of these distinctions. In intention, at least, it has been our purpose to point out "what is there" with respect to the distinction between essence and existence. This is not at all the same as a theory about, say, the ontological status of essences, e.g., whether or not they are eternal, created by God, etc. Furthermore, we have not argued that if a certain ontological (metaphysical and/or theological) position is assumed—and slyly assumed!—then these distinctions in the order of teaching and learning follow. No, rather, the argument has been that *this and that are necessary to the order of teaching and learning, and so much the worse for any ontological position incompatible with it.* As a rigorous test of our method, let us take an extreme example: Catholic education, in the "Catholic parochial school." What we are saying is that whatever is true in the philosophy of education, on the level of the order of teaching and learning, must be respected by Catholic schools; if not, then the Catholic school fails to live up to its own pretensions.

In the first place, the priority of parental rights over the school must be, and usually is, respected by the Catholic school. The Catholic parent, precisely because he is a Catholic, can be persuaded to send his child to a Catholic school. But the Catholic school would be violating the principle if it made use of the State to enforce its will.

Second, the Catholic school, too, must recognize the correct instrumental relations between knowing and doing. It cannot, and still remain a school, substitute worship and other kinds of "doings" for the "knowings" for which the school uniquely exists. Such doings are quite legitimate if they are "in addition to," but not a "substitute for." A teacher may create attitudes favorable to the Church provided they come with and from knowledge.

Third, the Catholic school, as any other school, must preserve its essential nature as a school, and not try to become something else. The school cannot try to be a church, or be like it. The principle here is this, that if x and y are really distinct, the attempt to make x into a y, or conversely, is a recipe for the perversion of both. This holds universally in the nature of things, even in the order of knowledge. For example, if one attempts to reduce logic to mathematics, or conversely, both are distorted. And so, in the relation of school and Church. The Catholic school must be *primarily* a place for knowing, to which doing is instrumental. The Church is *primarily* a place for doing (worship, prayer, etc.) and to which knowing (theology, etc.) is instrumental. It must be emphasized that the distinction does not imply a separation. There will be knowings and doings in both the school and the Church. But if the distinction between what is primary and what is secondary is broken down, then the uniqueness, the essential nature of each institution, is broken down.

The same analysis would hold for a Jewish Day School in relation to the Synagogue or Temple. What is true with respect to revelation, whether in Catholicism or Judaism, is not a problem of the order of teaching and learning. But whatever is true on the level of that order must be respected by any religious school. It is of interest to note that in the contemporary world the threat to the uniqueness of the school as an institution comes from secular rather than religious powers. Some secular educators would deny the priority of parental rights and, by making use of the law and power of the State, would force all children into nonreligious schools under the slogan of "nondivisiveness" in education. But this is just as questionable as it would be to force, by the power of the State, all children into parochial schools. The enlightened Catholic of today would go even further and hold that the Church should not use State power even to force Catholic children to go to Catholic schools.

Those who take their religion seriously, whether they be Christian, Jewish, Moslem, or other, recognize that religion and education cannot be separated. Down through the ages Judaism has been a way of life based upon a belief in the God of the Hebrew Scriptures and of his revelation to a certain people. To abstract and separate this from the education of the child is ultimately to cause the withering away of Judaism. The Communist countries are at least consistent in recognizing this and acting accordingly, for they know that in the long run the most efficacious way of destroying religion is to separate it from education. This is done through the power of the State, but it is no less efficacious in the long run if, through indifference or ignorance, those affiliated with Church, Synagogue, Mosque, etc., accomplish the same purpose voluntarily.

By making use of previous analyses, let us see why this is so. The foundation lies, once again, in the mutual instrumentalities between doing (conduct) and knowing, keeping in mind the distinction between what is primary and what is secondary in an institution. Religious institutions such as the Church, Synagogue, and Mosque, exist primarily for the purpose of doing—worship, prayer, mission work, etc. Such doing presupposes knowledge-claims; otherwise they become purely ideological for pragmatic and power purposes. The acquisition of such knowledge is the function of the school associated with the religious institution. It is logically impossible, by the law of noncontradiction, for an institution to have two primary aims. The religious knowledge obtained in the school will inform and make more meaningful the worship and prayer, for people will know better what *they* are *doing*. Conversely, the doing, i.e., the *practice* of the religion enables one better to know, for it *concretizes* that which one learns *about* in the school. Why is this so? To understand this let us turn again to the relation between essence and existence, sense and conceptual knowledge.

There are only two possible sources of knowledge—that which comes from sense experience and that which comes by special revelation from God. If God does not exist, then there is no revelation, hence there is only one source of knowledge. On the level of the order of teaching and learning alone, the question of God's existence cannot be determined one way or another. It is a problem on the level of the "order of being." However, what we can do at present is to show some of the educational implications if the ontological knowledge-claim of God's existence and His revelation is accepted. We shall do so by making use of those principles and distinctions which are "built-in of necessity" into the teaching-learning activities, *and which, as such, are independent of the question of whether or not God exists*. If God exists, then the existential encounter must be with God, man, and nature. If God does not exist, then such encounter is limited to the latter two.

On a purely secular level, as we have seen, there must be the kind of doing which is the existential encounter with nature and man in order to obtain the experience which is the foundation of all knowledge. Through existential experience we grasp the uniqueness and singularity of things. This experience and knowledge is much broader than the conceptual which is obtained from it by intellectual abstraction. If we had only conceptual knowledge we could never know any *thing* in the world, not even a particular person. Not only, then, does the dynamic action which is *doing* furnish us with the experience from which conceptual knowledge is obtained, but also it furnishes us with that additional and broader experience by which we can become acquainted with the singular existent. To use an example already given, one can study about the problem of Negroes by reading a book. This is chiefly intellectual activity. Also, one can *do* something, and go to a Negro section and see how they live—not "in general," but "right there." But even this doing never gets beyond that of the impartial, detached spectator. Another kind of doing is to live with them, with a white or darkened skin, and share their struggles. When one does this he is having an existential encounter with singular existents—not men in general, but with *this* landlord, *this* restaurant owner, *this* judge, etc. Such experience not only supplies additional knowledge, but it also points up and sharpens the knowledge obtained from a book. Even the language a person may use can be a witness to this. One may say, "In a sense I knew this, but I never quite realized it before." Behind the vagueness of the language lies a truth one is trying to express. There are the concepts of empathy and sympathy, but neither *is* a concept. In fact, when the feelings of sympathy and empathy—and, of course, they are not *mere* feelings—arise in a certain kind of existential encounter between persons, then they "know" in a way that cannot be exhausted by, or confined to, conceptual knowledge.

All of this should be taken into account in curriculum construction, and in this sense John Dewey and many others have been quite correct. But one must allow those who are not secula*rists* to be consistent, too, that they may carry out the same principles in man's existential encounter with God, and hence shape the school and construct the curriculum accordingly. Let us go back to the case of the Catholic church and school.

The Catholic school does not negate secular education. It quite consistently holds that while it is absolutely necessary, it is not sufficient. A school that is *secularistic* believes, quite consistently, too, and practically by definition, that secular education is, both necessary and sufficient. Secular education is, then, what they both have in common. What is unique to the Catholic school is that which it holds *in addition*, that God exists, that he has revealed himself through Jesus Christ, that such truths should be known by all men, for they are, at minimum, the intellectual key to salvation, etc. Hence, God, through Christ, founded the

Church, whose mission it is to bring God's truths to men, which truth could never be obtained through sense experience alone, or by reasoning and abstraction from it. Now, salvation is to be obtained not merely by knowing, but by doing—prayer, worship, rites, rituals, taking communion, going to confession, etc. (That non-Catholics can be "saved" too is true, but is not here relevant to our problem.) It is by such doing that one encounters Existence, God. Without Catholic education such doing is relatively abstracted from knowing. However, without the doing, for which the Church exists, the knowing would become sterile. There would be constant talk about, reading about, thinking about, having "ideas" about, God. But without any existential encounter through doing, God, in effect, is reduced from Existence to Idea. He becomes a concept, and it is only one step further to skepticism; for one can always ask whether or not the "idea" of God is any longer useful. Part of the history of modern theological skepticism is the history of the separation of education from Christianity. Catholicism recognizes this and quite consistently opposes such separation.

Furthermore in the Catholic school the curriculum, of necessity, provides for the theological knowledge that can inform worship and make it something other than random, arbitrary, or authoritarian doing. On the other hand, the school will insist upon the doing for which the Church exists, *for such doing provides the existential experience which gives content and substance to the knowing obtained in the school.* This is in part, but only in part, the meaning of the statement that "works" as well as "faith" are necessary. For "works" refers to a kind of religious doing; faith is a matter of intellectual consent through an act of the will.

We see that the mutual instrumentality of knowing and doing holds for the religious education in a Catholic school just as it holds for secular education. Of course, if God does not exist, there is no revelation; if there is no special revealed truth, there is nothing to know; and if there is no such knowing, then there can be no doing instrumental to it. In fact, the only thing to be *done* is, as the Marxist would say, to get rid of religion. However, as has been pointed out before, this is an ontological question, and not one of the order of teaching and learning. The principles of that order remain just what they are. What would change would be their applicability. If there is no existing God, then they would not be applicable to religious education.

And, now, finally to the reason why the instrumentality between knowing and doing is an important principle.

There must be some kind of unity in both knowledge and any curriculum. Kinds of knowledge, though distinguishable, are not unrelated absolutes. When one understands the manner in which they are related, then one understands the unity, the integration, of knowledge. A curriculum must have some unity, some integration, for it is a plan of studies, not a random or arbitrary selection of materials. What kinds and levels of integration are there?

Relevant to the order of teaching and learning there are three general kinds of integration: (1) integration on the level of knowledge alone; (2) integration on the level of doing and making; and (3) integration on the curricular level. We shall see that the curricular level mediates between the other two. We include in the second making as well as doing, for both are practical *activities* in contrast to knowing. Thus far, for the purpose of analysis we have stressed doing. Let us keep in mind that practical knowledge is still knowing, not doing or making. Knowing how to do something is practical knowing, but it is still knowing and not doing; the doing is the practice itself.

INTEGRATION OF KNOWLEDGE

Theoretical knowledge and practical knowledge can be integrated. On the theoretical level, there are also two kinds of integration. There is integration within a field of knowledge, and between fields of knowledge.

Even within a field of knowledge there is a division of labor in the activity of knowing. Physics is a kind of knowledge, marked off by its formal object or aspect from other kinds. Yet, within physics there are the divisions such as mechanics, electricity, heat, optics, etc. Operating on the nonarbitrary assumption, and for which there is some evidence, that a division of labor does not necessarily imply the same division in things, there will be an attempt to integrate these parts of physics. Some over-all "field theory" will be developed. The categories that unify physics will be, of course, categories of physics and not of any other kind of knowledge. Similarly for any other autonomous science. The categories of the theory of evolution have performed such a function in biology, but such categories are *of* and *within* biology.

The examples given have been those of the positive sciences, i.e., those sciences which can develop and have a certain autonomy of their own independent of any metaphysical or theological evidence. However, these various positive sciences are themselves but aspects of the physical world, hence they, too, may be integrated. The concepts or categories in terms of which the integration is made will, and must be, those of the positive sciences themselves. Such integration is for the most part always partial. The subject called "physical chemistry" is an example of such partial integration.

Attention should be called to the fact that because all of the positive sciences have a common method, namely, the "scientific method" or the "experimental method," this alone is not sufficient for integration. The end product of integration is itself knowledge. It is *what* is known, and this is something different from a method. The scientific method is a *means by which* a certain kind of knowledge is obtained. But the integration itself is done *by means of* concepts and categories obtained by the method.

There is another integrative level, that in which diverse kinds of knowledge are related not in terms of some formal object or aspect they share in common, but rather in reference to being or existence—even though the integration itself, being theoretical, is still on a conceptual level. This is the philosophical problem of discovering the relation between all kinds of knowledge, not just those which share a common method or are concerned with a certain limited kind or mode of existence. Such philosophical integration is of two kinds, depending upon whether the reference is to knowledge alone or to some kind of existence *about* which there is knowledge. If the integration is with respect to knowledge alone, then we have what is called "the order and integration of knowledge." If the integration is of the latter kind, then it is called by various names, depending upon the existence referred to, and is usually prefaced by the words "philosophy of." If it is history, then it is the philosophy of history; if it is nature, then it is the philosophy of nature—which is not quite the same thing as the "philosophy of science." Since these distinctions are rather abstract and presuppose perhaps a good deal of philosophical knowledge, it may be well to clarify them by giving some examples, which will show the grounds for the distinctions.

Let us consider first some examples of integration on the level of kinds of knowledge alone, without reference to existence. One would be the proposition: Mathematics is instrumental to, but not constitutive as evidence of, truths in physics. This proposition relates one kind of knowledge to another in terms of evidence. Second, it means that some mathematical truths *must* be relevant as evidence to some truth in physics, but which mathematical truths are relevant is determined by physics and not by mathematics. Another proposition: Logic is regulative of, but not constitutive as evidence of, physics. This proposition also relates one kind of knowledge to another. It means that logical truth cannot be used as evidence for, cannot be used to demonstrate or prove, any truth in physics. But it also means that logic nevertheless delimits what can be possibly, not actually, true in physics. Physics presupposes logic, but not conversely.

These propositions are presumably true, and are examples of the integration of knowledge *qua* knowledge, unconcerned with existence as such. It should be said that, for the purpose of illustration, it is the kind of proposition that is relevant to our problem, and not the question of whether it is true or false. Even if these propositions were false, then their contradictories or contraries would still be examples of the integration of knowledge.

The other kind of integration is always with reference to some kind of existence. Again, without prejudice to God's existence, for we are dealing with *all possible* alternatives, there are three general kinds—God, Man, and Nature. Hence, there are kinds of knowledge-claims called "Philosophy of God," "Philosophy of

Man," and "Philosophy of Nature." A note should be made of the change in terminology in recent times through the influence of Positivism. The "philosophy of nature" is really what was formerly called "natural science," i.e., the science of the *nature of things*, which requires both the ontological and phenomenological data of the positive sciences.

Consider the following propositions as examples of types of knowledge. First, the proposition: Any entity whose behavior is a function of volume is one having a definite size. This is a metaphysical proposition; in fact, one of special metaphysics, dealing with being as change, and not with being as being. The categories of "substance" and "quantity" are metaphysical categories. "Entity" is a category of substance, and "volume" and "size" are categories of quantity. The truth (or falsity) of this proposition can be known on the grounds of metaphysics *alone:* for what is related are the categories of substance and quantity, both of which are metaphysical (ontological) categories.

Let us now analyze another proposition: Molecules are entities whose behavior is a function of volume. What kind of a proposition is this? It is a proposition of physics as a positive science, and presumably true. Why is this so? In the first place, the term "molecule" is a concept of physics (or chemistry) as a positive science, i.e., as completely independent of the ontological. Theology *qua* theology, and metaphysics *qua* metaphysics, neither know, nor *can* know, anything about molecules. In fact, metaphysics *qua* metaphysics developed as a kind of knowledge-claim long before the idea of "molecule" was ever thought of, or the existence of molecules was discovered. The idea of a "molecule" is strictly one discovered through the researches of positive science. Furthermore, all the metaphysical reasoning man can do would not, and could not, lead him to this discovery. Such a discovery can only be accomplished through the use of the scientific method.

However, given the two propositions, one of (special) metaphysics, and the other of positive science, we can by logic alone deduce that: Molecules are entities having a definite size. Now, what kind of proposition is this? It is a proposition of the Philosophy of Nature, i.e., the science of the "nature of *things*."

Why is this so? Because the proposition relates a category of positive science, which from the standpoint of the ontological *alone* one could not know, with the metaphysical category of "quantity." For a proposition of this kind, then, there is evidence of two kinds that are necessary—metaphysics and that of positive science. Each enters *constitutively* as evidence into the proposition. Again, let it be noted that this is the case independently of whether or not the proposition is true. Even if one were to deny the truth of the proposition, it would have to be done in terms of another proposition which itself would be the result of an integration of the metaphysical and positive sciences.

The same kind of integration can occur with respect to man, or with respect to God. During the last century arguments about the nature of man, whether man is the product of Nature or God, were really arguments on the level of the "Philosophy of Man" and not at all on the level of metaphysics alone, or of positive science about man, alone. The proposition "Human intelligence is an effect of the creative power of nature," is a proposition of the philosophy of human nature. The reason is that the evidence, or the evidence-claim, lies in two other propositions, that human intelligence is an effect "higher" than its causes, and second, that any effect "higher" than its causes is due to the creative power of nature. The latter proposition is a metaphysical one having to do with the nature of causality. The former is a proposition of psychology as an experimental science, for metaphysics *qua* metaphysics has nothing to do with human intelligence as a kind of subject matter.

The integration consists in this, that when two kinds of knowledge are brought together, a hybrid kind of knowledge is formed. Such knowledge is not autonomous, but rather depends solely for its truth upon the evidence of the other two kinds of knowledge which *are* autonomous.

Again, let it be noted that the denial of the truth of the proposition of the philosophy of man that was used for the purpose of illustration does not allow one to escape from the problem of integration. One may argue that human intelligence is due to God's intervention through secondary causes, for it is an effect higher than its causes, and any effect higher than its causes must be due to an intervention from God. If so, then again a proposition of the philosophy of nature, as a knowledge-claim, is obtained by appealing to two kinds of evidence from two kinds of knowledge, the ontological, and psychology as a positive science.

It must be noted, however, that there are those who would deny that there is any such kind of integration at all. Either through an epistemological or a linguistic approach, they would argue that there can be no metaphysical propositions, hence no problem of their truth or falsity. From the standpoint of truth and falsity, metaphysical propositions are meaningless, although they may have "emotional" or some other kind of meaning. Now, such a thesis is not an alternative solution of any problem we are dealing with. Rather, the thesis eliminates the problem. In fact, from the standpoint of such a position there could be no problem such as this book deals with—the order of teaching and learning.

These two kinds of integration, that on the level of conceptual knowledge alone, and that on the level of knowledge with reference to some kind of existence, are both of a theoretical, not practical, nature. Even in case of reference to existence one never gets beyond the *idea* of existence, the *idea* of man, the *idea* of molecule or some other natural entity, or the *idea* of God.

The other kind of integration is that on the level of the "practical," that of knowing how to do, knowing how to make. A college of medicine aims to produce physicians who can diagnose and treat the ills of John Jones or Mary Smith; for "man in general" does not get sick. Yet, the college of medicine, as such, is a school devoted to the activities of teaching and learning. That is its function, and not primarily the cure of the ills of John Jones. That is the primary function of the hospital. The college and the hospital cooperate, of course; but that is only possible because there is a real distinction between them. The science of medicine is not an autonomous science such as, say, physics. Rather medicine integrates various theoretical kinds of knowledge, not for a theoretical, but for a practical purpose—knowing how to *do* something.

We are already acquainted with the distinction between primary and secondary in connection with the practical activity of making. A school of engineering exists primarily *not* to build bridges, among other things, but to teach students how to build them. Engineering is not an autonomous science. Rather, being practical, it integrates for a practical purpose kinds of knowledge that in themselves are not practical.

Whether integration is on a theoretical level—and there are two kinds there—or on a practical level, it is still integration of knowledge. The existential in its real being is not involved. The idea of existence is not existence. Knowing how to do something is knowing, not doing, and knowing how to make something is also knowing, and not making.

INTEGRATION OF DOING AND MAKING

Keeping in mind the mutual instrumentality of knowing and doing and making, we can now understand another way in which knowledge may be integrated. Spanning the Hudson River in New York is the George Washington Bridge. It exists, and as such can only be named. There can be no concept of any singular existent, and all existents are singular. Knowing how to build bridges in general is the kind of knowledge that can be taught and learned in an engineering school. Knowing how to build the George Washington Bridge cannot be learned in school, but rather "on the job." We will remember that the second kind of "know-how" actually transcends the first because such knowledge can only be acquired by an encounter with a given set of existential conditions—just these and no others. Now, instrumental to *this* building will be various kinds of knowledge—not only physics, chemistry, metallurgy, geology, mathematics, and all the other sciences usually associated with engineering, but also economics, politics, law, and perhaps even ethics.

These kinds of knowledge may be said to be integrated because they are related in a certain way. What integrates them is not knowledge, but rather a practical human purpose. But even this is only necessary, and not sufficient, for such can be said about any bridge "in general." In the case at hand *that which* integrates various kinds of knowledge is the actual, existing bridge itself. Since there is a development from potentiality to actuality, it would be more accurate to say that what integrates is the activity of building this particular bridge.

The example of the building of the George Washington Bridge is merely one illustration out of innumerable others. If the activity of making can integrate, so can the activity of *doing*. When a physician treats the health of John Jones, then John Jones can be said to be the existent that integrates knowledge—for many kinds of knowledge may be brought to bear upon his case, not only anatomy, physiology, pathology, bacteriology, etc., but also perhaps psychology and sociology. Similarly with the kind of doing that is "legislation," the creation of new laws (jurisprudence, the philosophy of law, is something different). In constructing a tax law the legislative branch of government must bring to bear various kinds of knowledge—economics, political science, sociology, ethics, etc.—upon a *given* existential situation in a particular place and (within limits) at a particular time.

If, in actual doing and making, an existent can be that which integrates, then the same would be true on the religious plane. From the standpoint of serious theism, knowing about God is never sufficient. There must be an existential encounter, and that is only possible by doing something. Hence, Judaism is a way of life. A Moslem will wash, pray, face Mecca, or go to Mecca. The Christian will pray, go to Church, go to communion, go to confession, etc. Knowing the Hebrew Scriptures, the Koran, or the New Testament and the theology of the Church is necessary and instrumental to intelligent action, but it is not sufficient. Practical doing, action, is also necessary; and it is God who exists, I AM WHO AM, that is the integration factor, just as John Jones can be said to be the existential integrating factor for a practicing physician.

On the other hand, if God does not exist and religion remains practical activity, then it must be that of making and not doing. This was the thesis of Ludwig Feuerbach in the first part of the 19th century, and almost all contemporary atheism, and naturalistic and materialistic explanations of religion, have been footnotes to, or elaborations of, his *The Essence of Christianity*. In doing, one perfects a "nature" that is given. The veterinarian helps the dog get well. And so does the physician treating a person. Neither the dog nor the person is created by the practitioner. On the other hand, in making something man creates an artifact, the very nature of which is a human creation, for the artifact had no nature prior to the creative action of man. Now, if God does not really exist, then only the *idea* of God has being. Since the idea has no objective foundation, then its generation must be ascribed to psychological and/or social conditions. Instead of, "in the beginning created He him," we now have "created HIM he," for God and the gods have always been human artifacts created for a purpose.

Both Marx and Lenin, quite logically, raised a question about the purpose of such creativity. To make a bridge or an engine is one thing, but to fabricate gods and then believe that one is *not* making them is simply a form of self-delusion. It is a form of narcotic which man takes in order to deaden the pains that come from living in a "class" society. To the degree that class exploitation is eliminated and communism is approached, then religion will gradually wither away, for no longer will there be any need for a spiritual narcotic. Hence Lenin, and again quite logically, criticized both Gorki and Lunacharsky for being "god creators" when they suggested that even for socialist purposes, perhaps, the idea of God might have a function. No, the task is to get on with the class struggle.

A different approach was taken by many in the West. The argument, in brief, was that a little bit of the narcotic that is religion can do no harm if it is controlled. In fact, it may make life a little easier to bear. This is the case with, say, drinking. Of course, it can be overdone, and one can go to excess in religion, too. The orthodox Protestant has often accused the "liberal" Protestant of tending toward this view, hence there has arisen a rather strange name for it, "religious atheism." Also, there has crept into journalism, at least, the notion of "theology without God." Apparently, a contradiction can only be expressed contradictorily. Since those of such persuasion also speak of "existential encounter" in expounding their antitheological theology, the ghost of Lenin would perhaps remind them that what they are really encountering is their own lonely existence, that in trying to have and not have authentic religion they succeed only in intensifying the causes which have long ago led to such an egoistic, negativistic, and antisocial atheism—all of which at best is boredom in despair, and at its worst is a form of spiritual onanism.

If God is only a man-created idea, then there is only secular doing; in which case the Church in its historical and ontological being not only becomes unnecessary because there is no special kind of authoritative theological knowledge to be taught or learned, but also it is a social obstacle because it tends to be a "divisive" influence in a "democratic" society. If there is no authoritative theological knowledge, then there can be none to be taught or learned. Hence, under the guise of doing what is impossible, the religious school in effect only creates hostile or antisocial attitudes.

HOW A CURRICULUM INTEGRATES KNOWING WITH DOING AND MAKING

We have now seen how there can be integration on two levels, that of knowing, and that of practical activity, i.e., doing and making. Knowing is primarily an intellectual activity, whether it be that of knowing what, how, that, or when. It is primarily also an individual activity, and not institutional. Doing and making are activities involving the *whole* person, and can be either of an individual or of an institutional nature. Furthermore, we have seen that each is instrumental to the other. Knowing without doing or making is sterile and lacks efficacy; doing and making without knowledge are random activities unworthy of the name "human." Now, the question arises as to how to get the two together. What is it that can integrate knowing and practical activities? Neither one can do it alone. This integrating function is performed by and through the teachers, and by the school as an institution. More exactly, it is done by the curriculum of the school, and the special curriculum by means of which the teachers teach. Let us see how this is accomplished.

Before doing so, however, a question may be raised. Since the aim of the student is to know, and the aim of teaching is that of helping the student to know, have we not "loaded" our thesis on the side of knowing rather than that of practical activity? Is this not an arbitrary assumption smuggled in? What is the evidence? It is this: knowing *qua* knowing is a unique human activity. Schools are not constructed upon the knowledge that human beings and other creatures share in common. On the other hand, in abstraction from knowing, doing *qua* doing and making *qua* making, are not unique human activities. A dog mates and reproduces. A bird builds a shelter (nest). Man, too, does the same basic things. *What is uniquely human is the kind and nature of the doing and making, namely, that which is informed by that kind of knowing which is distinctively human.*

How then does a curriculum integrate? The question is not how knowing *qua* knowing integrates knowing and practice. Knowledge can integrate only knowledge. But then, even that is vague, and not quite exact, and in any case is not the whole story.

The secret of how a curriculum can integrate knowing with practice is this: an existential category as well as a knowledge category can integrate on the curricular level. We use the word "category" to refer either to a concept or a name, the distinction to be understood in the context in which it is found. Let us recall that an "essential nature" can be grasped, however incompletely, by a concept. Any existent, finite or infinite, can only be named. There is no concept of St. Francis, George Washington, Hitler, or M. Gandhi, but there can be conceptual knowledge *about* them, and this can be taught. An existent can only have an "image," it can not be conceptualized. This is the reason why in advertising and public relations work there is talk about the "image" of the U. S. Steel Co., the "image" of a senator up for re-election, etc.

Even if we run the risk of excessive repetition, we must call attention to a former caveat, namely, that the concept of existence is a concept only, and is not the same as that which is referred to by an existential name. Colors and numbers, for example, can be conceptualized, they cannot be named. "Red" has being, and there is a concept of red; but "red" does not exist, only red *things* exist. Numbers have being of a kind, and there is the concept of "number"; but numbers do not exist, only *things* that are numbered. However, men exist and hence have to be named; but there is also the concept, the idea, of man. Hence, the *idea* of man, of men as existents, can be used as an integrating factor in knowledge, which kind of knowledge, as we have seen, has been called the "philosophy of man," or the "philosophy of human nature." However, this is not the same as using an existential "name" as an integration entity in a curriculum. For on a theoretical level even the "philosophy of man" can never get beyond *the idea of man as existing*. On the other hand, when the sixth grade teacher teaches about Australia, it is not the "idea of Australia" that is the integrating factor, but rather the name that refers to the existent. In fact, there literally is no such thing as the "idea" of Australia, *although there can be the "idea" of Australia as existing.*

The same analysis holds true with respect to teaching about God on the level of reason alone. It is worth mentioning this fact because of its relevance to the teaching of courses called "natural theology" or the "philosophy of religion." God, as an existent, can only be named. This is recognized in classical theism, philosophical and biblical. St. Thomas ends his arguments for God's existence on the level of reason alone by referring to what men call "God." In the Old Testament God is not so much conceptualized as referred to by the phrase I AM WHO AM. Now, the "idea of God as existing" is not at all the same as the "name of God who exists." On the level of reason alone, that of conceptualizing, all one can ever know is *the idea of an existing God*. Only by an existential encounter with God can one know God, He Who is called by that name. And, as we have seen, for that kind of knowledge *doing* is necessary, and not merely conceptual knowing. The existential comes by way of special revelation, for it is concerned with what God *does* and what man must *do*, each in relation to the other, the I-THOU relation. Without this, there is a reduction of God to a philosophical idea.

Recent studies in the philosophy of education of an existentialist kind, together with the educational philosophy of John Dewey and his followers, have always had a healthy effect in emphasizing action and doing in correcting an overemphasis on the intellectual stemming from Hegelianism, which tends to dissolve everything into ideas. "Existence" cannot be reduced to idea alone, to become merely another predicate. Of course, a correction in emphasis can itself become so absolute that, by the irony of the Hegelian dialectic, an opposite error is generated. In this case the emphasis on existence becomes *"existentialism,"* with the implication, implicit or explicit, of the denial of essence. It is in this sense that contemporary existentialism can be criticized as inadequate, although at the same time one can be sympathetic with its criticism of all kinds of essentialism. The priority of existence does not require the elimination of essence; rather it presupposes it. The correction for an excessive intellectualism need not be an anti-intellectualism.

It has been pointed out that a curriculum can integrate knowing with doing and making because it can use existential categories as well as knowledge categories. As an example of the former we referred to "Australia." Now, it may be said that although this is an existential category, it is not clear how this is related to any kind of action on the part of the student. Even though such a category brings together various kinds of knowledge, it is *done* by the teacher or a book. Is not the student just as passive as if he were studying a nonexistential subject such as mathematics? There is no existential doing, and hence no integration.

This is true, but it is not the whole story. The criticism points up the necessity for further clarification. A curriculum, being a means, is partially determined by environmental circumstances. These same circumstances delimit what is possible, practical, and expedient. A curricular program may be limited by a school budget. The students lack the opportunity to *do* and *make* simply because of a lack of financial means—e.g., a lack of money for band instruments.

A curricular program may be limited by the geographical location of the school. There may be no mountains near by to which the students can go to make an "existential encounter." They may be limited (1) to the "idea" of mountains, or (2) to an existential name, the "Rocky Mountains" or the "Alps."

The state of technology at any given time may be a further limitation in a curricular program. Not long ago a curricular program for a rural student may have included the kind of doing which was taking a trip with his "social science" class to the big city twenty miles away. By doing so he would study this city, and not merely learn out of books and lectures about cities "in general." The student today is not so limited. He now may go with a group of students to Washington, New York, to the art centers of Europe, etc., all made possible by the jet plane. At present he cannot go to the moon or Mars, and since there can be no existential encounter with these singular existents, he is limited to their "names," *about which* he studies in school.

In the light of these samples of the kinds of limitations on a curricular program, we can now make the following distinctions with respect to existential encountering as instrumental to knowing. First, there is that which is desirable but impossible. In a curriculum in astronomy it would be, perhaps, desirable, to take a group of students to Mars. It is not now possible; but if it ever becomes so in the future, then it may be desirable. The term "possibility" here has a temporal connotation. That which is "logically" impossible could never be desirable.

Second, there is that which is desirable and possible, but impractical. The example of Australia would be an illustration of this. A group of students could be flown to Australia, and, all other things being equal, it may be said to be desirable. However, the qualification signifies its impracticality, for the time and expense may not make it worthwhile. The limitation here is not merely an economic one which might be overcome. There is the question of time and values. If time is spent doing this, then there will not be (curricular) time to do something else. Hence, there is the question of value in the use of time. The pace of action can be quickened by faster planes, but presumably time itself cannot be increased in any meaningful sense relevant to our problem.

Third, there is that which is desirable, possible, practical, and expedient, e.g., going to a nearby factory or slum area as a project. Like any other means a curriculum cannot be blue-printed; it can only be generally described. But it is this that a teacher or a school will wisely attempt to determine. What is possible may be relatively easy to determine. It will be more difficult to discover what is practicable, for desirability in the abstract is not sufficient. This determination ultimately will be made in terms of the values involved. This is really the crucial issue in determining projects for students. And at this point there is required the further specification of the general principle that doing is instrumental to knowing and learning. What has to be determined is what kind of doing, under what kind of conditions and limitations, most effectively contributes to a student's learning. This the teacher cannot learn in teacher education. For a given curriculum is as much a humanly created artifact as a bridge; and, just as with the engineer, the teacher will have to learn something when he gets to his "on-the-job training" that he could never learn in a college of education.

In passing it may be noted that existential experience for the student will always have the natural limitation of space and time. Since all finite beings come into existence and perish, he can only experience that which exists contemporaneously with his action. A history class can arrange an interview with a living ex-president of the United States, but not now with F. D. Roosevelt. What the student will be limited to are the existential remains of the past. He will also be limited by space, and in two ways. A student is a product of *this* particular bit of geography, having *this* culture and not that. What is the experience that a native from India has when he comes to the United States, registers in hotels, and eats in restaurants? The blonde, blue-eyed student in Omaha can never know through an existential encounter because he cannot be who he is and at the same time be someone else. He can try to transcend himself and his culture, and it is good if he does so. But this is what one does when one cannot directly know through an existential encounter.

When it comes to outer and not merely earthly space, a further built-in limitation is discovered. Even if there are intelligent beings on planets of suns in remote galaxies, an existential encounter would presumably be impossible. For we are told that even in the attempt to communicate by radio beams, if a question is asked the reply could not be received by the sender, but only by someone living generations hence.

It is worthwhile mentioning all these limitations because man, with his Dionysian tendencies is apt to forget his finite nature and assume that by increased practical activities he can do and know more than he is able. He either deifies himself or assumes that in progressively conquering the world he better understands it. The fact that there is inner as well as outer space is dismissed by some as an old-fashioned and out-dated idea. This may or may not be so, for what is necessary may not be sufficient. Carried over into education this view can create questionable attitudes, as in curriculum planning when an excessive amount of doing in the way of projects is included on the assumption that there is an equivalent amount of learning. Taken literally, this assumption would amount to practically identifying doing and knowing, instead of recognizing the instrumental relation.

It may be of interest to note how a religious school deals with these limitations. Since the majority of such schools are Catholic, we may use these for illustrative purposes. Insofar as the secular part of Catholic education is concerned, it has the same problems and can only offer the same solutions as a school that is purely secular. However, with respect to the "holy" and not merely the "secular," the limitations we have mentioned can be transcended— and it is to be understood that here we are not concerned with the truth or falsity of Catholicism, but only with the "logic" of it. Since an existential encounter can only occur with an existent contemporaneous with one's action, it is always possible to make an existential encounter with God. But this is only a possibility in the abstract, for there is an impassable gap, from the standpoint of man alone, between the infinite and the finite. This was transcended, so to speak, by the Incarnation, in which God became man in Jesus Christ, and upon whom the Holy Catholic Church was founded. Jesus as a man died, but as the Christ He is and always will be living. Hence, with respect to God and Christ it is possible for anyone at any time to have an existential encounter with God through Christ and the Church by certain kinds of doings and knowings.

It is sometimes said by materialists that seventeenth and eighteenth century deism was the first step toward modern atheism. They are correct. For the essence of deism consisted in denying Christ and revelation through Christ. God was rendered remote, and served chiefly the philosophical function of "first cause." Such a god cannot be existentially encountered. Hence, God as existing, tended to be reduced to the *idea* of God existing, and finally merely to an existing idea of God in the minds of man. That the latter is all that God is or ever has been was precisely the thesis of Ludwig Feuerbach in the nineteenth century, and one that has been the basis of atheism in its contemporary development. The contemporary naturalist or materialist does not at all deny that there exists the *idea* of God as existing; what is denied is God as existing.

The Catholic school perhaps runs less risk than some others in confusing knowing with doing or making. For if knowing were identified with doing, there would be no need for the Catholic school, and if knowing were identified with making, then there would be need neither for school nor Church.

On a purely secular level the curriculum of any school whatever must recognize the various kinds of restrictions on human doing and making and what can be learned by means of existential encountering. The latter is necessary and important and yet difficult to achieve through a curricular program. However, the school need not suffer because of this. It can perfect itself insofar as it is possible by keeping the following in mind. First, since, for the school, knowing and learning are primary, and doing and making are secondary and instrumental, this must be reflected in, and not distorted by the curriculum. Second, if so, then curricular planning will require a very careful and prudential selection of practical activities to be performed by students, compatible with and efficaciously instrumental to the specific kind of knowledge for which the curriculum exists. Third, from the standpoint of the *being* of a person it is knowing that makes unique human doing and making; *and not conversely*. Hence, a curriculum exists primarily for knowing.

This fact is most important of all, and the foundation of its truth lies in human *being*, not merely human purpose. Humans share with animals and other creatures the practical activities of doing and making. If such doing and making is qualitatively, and not merely quantitatively, superior to that of other creatures, it is because men have that which is not shared with other creatures;

and that is the potentiality of reasoning on a conceptual level, thus enabling man to develop theoretical kinds of knowledge which can inform not only those practical activities we have in common with other creatures but also those that are uniquely human.

Were it not for the intellectual ability to reason, to conceptualize, man would not only be subject to the spatio-temporal limitations of all finite existence, but he would also be a victim of them. With this ability man can literally transcend those limitations, not only by the fact that he knows them, which an animal can not know, but also in his doings and making. This is in a good part the basis of man's creativity. For example, he can create elements unknown to Nature. In doing so he participates in Nature's creativity by being a part of Nature, while at the same time transcending it.

Were it not for the intellectual ability to reason, to conceptualize, even that experience which is nonconceptual could not be informed and understood. Feelings, emotions, and experiences from existential encounters in the natural world are shared by animals and human beings. What lifts men up to become something more than themselves as human beings is the theoretical knowings, that come, to a large extent, from conceptualizing.

All this, however different in manner and mode of expression, must be recognized and reflected in the curriculum of any school, at any time, and at any place.

Index

Absolutes, use of, 127–128
Academic freedom, 65, 69–72, 75–77, 90; infringement of, 77; nature of, 65
Academic imperialism, 36
Acquaintance, knowledge by, 5, 6, 166
American Historical Association, Report of, 150–151
Antieducation, 127
Antiteaching, 101, 114–116, 135
Art, as moralism, 145
Artifact, 134
Arts: fine, 134–141, 143; use, 134, 141–147
Aschner, M. J., 21
Asymmetry, 8–12, 16–17
Atheism, 87, 184–185, 191
Authority, 16–17; analysis of, 2

Castell, Alburey, 8n., 25–27, 42, 43, 44, 46, 47
Catholicism, 115, 174–175, 191
Causation, 17–18
Cause: efficient, 20, 59, 83, 94, 148–193; final, 20; formal, 20, 82–147; material, 20, 58–81, 83
Causes, the traditional four, 17, 19–20

Common good, ethical meaning of, 45–46
Communism, 113, 172, 184
Concepts, 85–86, 88, 95, 115–116, 164–166, 186–187
Conceptualization, 166, 186–187, 193
Conditioning, 61–63, 88, 111, 149
Course, 91, 116, 120, 152, 155; kinds of knowledge in, 28; meaning of; 41; –subject distinction, 124; why of, 29–32
Creativity, 98–102, 144–145, 193; purpose of, 184
Curriculum, 21, 28, 38, 53, 91, 116, 120, 123, 134, 137–140, 146–147; constant factors in, 152; determinants of, 151–153, 188; and efficient causation, 148–193; importance of, 148; integrating by, 185–193; integration of, 176; intentionality of, 154–156; liberal, 28; limitations on, 188–191

Dewey, John, 60, 127, 167–169, 174, 187
Dialectical materialism, 109, 111–112, 122, 141, 169

195

Doing, 134–135; instrumentality of, 157–170, 172–176; kinds of, 159, 166–167, 174; knowing and, 157–170, 172–176, 185–193; in learning, 90–91; and making, 182–185; nature of, 91, 185–186; priority of, 169; proper and improper, 158
Dualism, 158
Duty, 66–67; freedom and, 69–74, 77–79

Education: Catholic, 115, 164, 171, 174–175, 191–192; elementary, 47; Nazi, 63–64; priorities in, 33, 163, 164; progressive, 112, 155, 169; religion in, 171–175; rungs in the ladder of, 42–46; secular, 172, 174–175; technical, 42, 44–45
  See also Higher education; Liberal education
Empiricism, 157
Ends, 15, 131–132; esthetic, 138, 145; immediate and remote, 19–57, 152; logical and psychological, 22–23
Equality, educational, 75
Essence, 188; distinction between existence and, 165, 169, 170; knowledge as, 14; meaning of, 165
Essentialism, 169
Esthetics, 126, 136–140, 142–143, 145–146
Ethics, 123–134, 145–146; teaching of, 86–87
Existence: act of, 165–166, 168; kinds of, 178; nature of, 188
Existential, the, relevance of, to teaching process, 12-13, 173–174, 188, 192
Existentialism, 14, 169, 188
Experience: existential and conceptual, 168–169; knowledge from, 5–6, 143; in learning, 157, 160–161, 164, 166, 190; meaning of, 67, 168; sense, 157, 160, 168

Fact, 134

Falsehoods, teaching of, 63–64, 76–77
Feeling, esthetic, 136
Feuerbach, Ludwig, 183, 192
Freedom, academic, 65, 69–72, 75–77, 90
Freud, S., 105, 106, 108

Genetic fallacy, 114
God: creation of, 87, 184; defined, 165; existence of, 168, 173, 178, 187, 192; existential encounter with, 173, 174–175, 183, 187, 191, 192
Gowin, D. B., 22

Hegelianism, 188
Higher education, 22; function of, 7–8
History, 123; importance of knowledge of, 43–44
How, the, of teaching, 20, 30, 33–34, 41, 56–57
Hutchins, Robert, 150–151

Idealism, 158
Ideas, 187
Ideology, 16, 33, 56, 62, 104, 111–113, 133; personal, 107–108
Indoctrination, 4, 33, 114
Induction, 44
Instrumentalism, 127–128, 130
Integration: curricular, 176; of doing and knowing, 185–193; of doing and making, 182–185; of knowledge, 176–182; levels of, 176
Intellectualism, 155, 166
Intelligence, 89, 158–159
Intuition, knowledge by, 5, 6

Judgment, 95–96
Justice, 46, 65, 67–69

Know-how, 42, 182; kinds of, 143
Knowing: distinguished from being, 85–88; integration of doing with, 185–193; know-how and, 144; means of, 88–91; mutuality of doing with, 185–193; nature of, 84–88, 91, 185

Index

Knowledge: by acquaintance, 5, 6, 166; change in, 153; conceptual, 164–165; distinguished from curriculum category, 25, 27, 51, 155; esthetic, 140; ethical, 130, 132, 142; as the formal cause, 82–147; integration of, 176–182; kinds of, 5–8, 13–14, 15, 28, 115–122, 142–143; order of, 118, 133, 145; philosophical, 51–53; practical, 126–134; relevant meaning of, 84–85; sources of, 157, 173; in technology, 142–143, 145; theological, 185; theoretical, 122–126, 142, 165–166

Law: natural, doctrine of, 68; positive, 67, 68, 70, 124–125
Learning: creative, 99–100, 169–170; as a diadic relation, 59; doing in, 90–91; formalized, 59–60; knowing vs. doing in, 157; means of, 91–94; priorities in process of, 160–161; purpose of, 20–21, 22; psychology of, 22–23; relationship of teaching to, 8–9; three senses of, 27, 32–33; trial and error, 6; two senses of, 8n., 26–27, 60–61
Lenin, 87, 184
Liberal education, 30–31, 32–34, 38, 41, 75, 123, 133–134, 146–147, 152; nature of, 42–49, 51, 54–55
Logic, 22, 50, 56, 88, 90

Man: philosophy of, 180, 187; uniqueness of, 158, 164, 186, 193
Marxism, 108–114, 122, 169
Materialism, 68–69, 109–112, 122, 141, 158–159, 169
Means, 15, 132; accidental, 149–150; alternative, 33–34; contingent, 60, 91; distinctions among, 84–94; ends as, 24; general vs. specific, 34–35; moral, 133; necessary, 34, 60, 91, 149; the teacher as, 60, 149; technology as, 145

Mental hygiene, 107
Metaphysics, 13, 122, 167, 179–180
Moral, the, distinguished from the ethical, 127–134

Naturalism, 68–69, 158
Nature, philosophy of, 179
Nihilism, 52, 63; esthetic, 137–138, 140; ethical, 45, 128, 133, 138
Nominalism, 88, 89, 91
Nonsense, teaching of, 63–64
Norms, 39–40, 46, 55, 139

Objects, existential and formal, 121–122
Ontology, 50, 68–69, 89, 140–141, 146
Ordering, kinds of, 117
Orders: knowledge, 118–120, 133, 145; relations among, 115–118; teaching and learning, 102–105

Pan-psychism, 167
Parents: duty of, 74; rights of, 170–172
Pedagogy, 15, 27, 60–61
Person, the, natural relations of, 105–110
Philosophizing, 56
Philosophy, 16, 178
Philosophy: need to know, 31, 33–34, 41, 44, 53–56, 90; of . . . , 51, 180; requirements for teaching, 35–39
Physicalism, 88, 89, 91
Positivism, 68, 103–104, 179
Power, 45–46, 55
Priorities in education, 33, 160–161, 163, 164; temporal and logical, 47–48
Progressivists, 150
Project method, 155, 161–162, 189–190
Propositionless theology, 87
Propositions, 85; *of* and *about*, 37–38, 155–156; truth and falsity of, 76–77, 95–97, 110–111, 114–115, 125, 181
Prudence, 76–77

Psychology, 106–107
Purpose, *see* Ends
Rationalism, 105–108, 157–158
Rationality, 110
Realism, 84, 141
Reductionism, 63, 157–158
Relations: diadic, 3–4, 12, 13, 15, 16, 59, 87; among kinds of knowledge, 118–122; among the three orders, 115–118; asymmetrical, 8–12; feeling-intellect, 136; individual, 105; means–end, 131–132; moral, 58–81; psychological, 107–110; student–curriculum, 153; teacher–student, 58–81; theory of, 3–14; transitive and intransitive, 12–14; triadic, 3–4, 12, 13, 59, 87
    See also Teaching relation
Religion, 171–176; doing in, 175, 183–185; and education, 171–173; teaching of, 87
Research, knowledge through, 6–7
Revelation, 83, 168, 172–174
Right, defined, 66–67
Rights: absolute, 68; forfeit of, 71–73; natural, 66–69, 71–72, 74, 80; positive, 66–67, 70, 73, 80; priorities of, 170–172
Ryle, Gilbert, 22

Scheffler, Israel, 22
Scholasticism, 89
School: conflict in, 39; limitations of, 170; purpose of, 29, 107–108; uniqueness of, 163, 170–172
Schooling, 59; equality of, 75; purpose of, 23
Science, 83
Sciences: applied, 141–147; moral, 126–127, 133; positive, 177, 179–180; social, 101, 124, 126; theoretical, 121, 144
Skill, 142, 143
Smith, B. Othanel, 22
Social sciences, 101, 124, 126
Soviet Union, 87, 111–113, 141
Student: conflicting ends of, 23, 24–25, 27–29; duties of, 70–73, 75; as efficient cause, 149; freedom of, 69; learning from, 9–10; as a material cause, 59–60; relations of, with curriculum, 153; rights of, 70, 80–81
Subjectivism, 55, 84, 97, 101–102, 139–141
Subjects, 124

Teach, two senses of, 27, 60–61
Teacher: duties of, 74–75, 77–79; as efficient cause, 59; function of, 98, 149, 152–153; purpose of, 97–98; requirements of, 35–39, 80, 134; rights of, 80
Teaching: causes of ineffective, 28–29; creative, 100–101, 169–170; importance of, 7–8; means of, 91–94; nature of, 87, 90; purpose of, 21, 22
Teaching activity: distinctions important to, 84–94; formalized, 4, 59, 60, 91–92, 152
Teaching relation: asymmetry of, 8–12; characteristics of, 3–17; corruption of, 15–17, 98; transitivity of, 12–14
Technocracy, 146
Technology, 141, 144–146; kinds of knowledge in, 142–143
Totalitarianism, 52
Transitivity, 12–14, 17
Trial and error, learning by, 6
Truth, 118; ideological determination of, 104–105, 111, 113; nature of, 94–105
Truths: selected, 76–77; teaching of, 63–64

Voluntarism, 52, 89

Weltanschauungs, 107, 108
What, the, of teaching, 5, 20, 30, 103
When, in education, 41, 46–47, 70
Whitehead, A. N., 167
Who, the, of teaching, 5, 20, 30, 33–34, 41, 56–57, 62
Why: curricular, 32, 35, 37; kinds of getting to know, 49–52; philosophical, 29–32, 35, 38–39; of teaching, 20, 43